180 Days of SCIENCE
for Fourth Grade

D0733064

Author
Lauren Homayoun

SHELL EDUCATION

Earth & Space
Life
Physical

Publishing Credits

Corinne Burton, M.A.Ed., *Publisher*
Conni Medina, M.A.Ed., *Managing Editor*
Emily R. Smith, M.A.Ed., *Content Director*
Shaun Bernadou, *Art Director*
Lynette Ordoñez, *Editor*

Image Credits

P.157 Kim Britten/Shutterstock; p.107 USGS/Corbis via Getty Images; all other images from iStock and/or Shutterstock.

Standards

© 2014 Mid-continent Research for Education and Learning (McREL)
NGSS Lead States. 2013. Next Generation Science Standards: For States, By States.
Washington, DC: The National Academies Press.

For information on how this resource meets national and other state standards, see pages 10–13. You may also review this information by visiting our website at www.teachercreatedmaterials.com/administrators/correlations/ and following the on-screen directions.

Shell Education

A division of Teacher Created Materials
5301 Oceanus Drive
Huntington Beach, CA 92649-1030
www.tcmpub.com/shell-education

ISBN 978-1-4258-1410-6
©2018 Shell Educational Publishing, Inc.

Table of Contents

Introduction

With today's science and technology, there are more resources than ever to help students understand how the world works. Information about science experiments you can do at home is widely available online. Many students have experience with physics concepts from games.

While students may be familiar with many of the topics discussed in this book, it is not uncommon for them to have misconceptions about certain subjects. It is important for students to learn how to apply scientific practices in a classroom setting and within their lives.

Science is the study of the physical and natural world through observation and experiment. Not only is it important for students to learn scientific facts, but it is important for them to develop a thirst for knowledge. This leads to students who are anxious to learn and who understand how to follow practices that will lead them to the answers they seek.

The Need for Practice

To be successful in science, students must understand how people interact with the physical world. They must not only master scientific practices but also learn how to look at the world with curiosity. Through repeated practice, students will learn how a variety of factors affect the world in which they live.

Understanding Assessment

In addition to providing opportunities for frequent practice, teachers must be able to assess students' scientific understandings. This allows teachers to adequately address students' misconceptions, build on their current understandings, and challenge them appropriately. Assessment is a long-term process that involves careful analysis of student responses from discussions, projects, or practice sheets. The data gathered from assessments should be used to inform instruction: slow down, speed up, or reteach. This type of assessment is called *formative assessment*.

How to Use This Book

Weekly Structure

All 36 weeks of this book follow a regular weekly structure. The book is divided into three sections: Life Science, Physical Science, and Earth and Space Science. The book is structured to give students a strong foundation on which to build throughout the year. It is also designed to adequately prepare them for state standardized tests.

Each week focuses on one topic. Day 1 sets the stage by providing background information on the topic that students will need throughout the week. In Day 2, students analyze data related to the topic. Day 3 leads students through developing scientific questions. Day 4 guides students through planning a solution. Finally, Day 5 helps students communicate results from observations or investigations.

 Day 1—Learning Content: Students will read grade-appropriate content and answer questions about it.

 Day 2—Analyzing Data: Students will analyze scientific data and answer questions about it.

 Day 3—Developing Questions: Students will read a scenario related to the topic, answer questions, and formulate a scientific question about the information.

 Day 4—Planning Solutions: Students will read a scenario related to the topic, answer questions, and develop a solution or plan an investigation.

 Day 5—Communicating Results: Students accurately communicate the results of an investigation or demonstrate what they learned throughout the week.

Three Strands of Science

This book allows students to explore the three strands of science: life science, physical science, and earth and space science. Life science teaches students about the amazing living things on our planet and how they interact in ecosystems. Physical science introduces students to physics and chemistry concepts that will lay the groundwork for deeper understanding later in their education. Earth and space science familiarizes students with the wonders of the cosmos and the relationships between the sun, Earth, moon, and stars.

How to Use This Book *(cont.)*

Weekly Topics

The following chart shows the weekly focus topics that are covered during each week of instruction.

Unit	Week	Science Topic
Life Science	1	Vertebrates and Invertebrates
	2	Land and Water Animals
	3	Plant Structures
	4	Nocturnal Animals
	5	How Birds Fly
	6	How Animals Use Their Legs
	7	How Fish Breathe Underwater
	8	Sight
	9	Smell
	10	Hearing
	11	How Animals Change Their World
	12	How Humans Change Our World
Physical Science	1	Speed and Energy
	2	Converting Potential Energy to Kinetic Energy
	3	Why Do Light Bulbs Get Hot?
	4	Converting Electricity into Sound
	5	How Does a Hairdryer Dry Hair?
	6	Energy Transfer in Collisions
	7	Collisions Can Cause Objects to Change Direction
	8	What Kind of Light Bulbs Are the Most Energy-Efficient?
	9	Waves
	10	Morse Code
	11	Sending Messages Over Long Distances
	12	How Light Helps Us See
Earth and Space Science	1	Earthquakes
	2	Patterns in Rock Formation
	3	Learning from Fossils in Rock Formations
	4	How Does Erosion Happen?
	5	Water Erosion
	6	Wind Erosion
	7	Topographic Maps
	8	Volcanoes and Earthquakes
	9	The Cost and Benefits of Dams
	10	Wind Power
	11	Reducing the Impact of Tsunamis
	12	Predicting Volcanic Eruptions and Earthquakes

How to Use This Book *(cont.)*

Best Practices for This Series

- Use the practice pages to introduce important science topics to your students.

- Use the Weekly Topics chart on page 5 to align the content to what you're covering in class. Then, treat the pages in this book as jumping off points for that content.

- Use the practice pages as formative assessment of the science strands and key topics.

- Use the weekly themes to engage students in content that is new to them.

- Encourage students to independently learn more about the topics introduced in this series.

- Lead teacher-directed discussions of the vocabulary and concepts presented in some of the more complex weeks.

- Support students in practicing the varied types of questions asked throughout the practice pages.

- When possible, have students participate in hands-on activities to answer the questions they generate and do the investigations they plan.

Using the Resources

An answer key for all days can be found on pages 194–207. Rubrics for Day 3 (developing questions), Day 4 (planning solutions), and Day 5 (communicating results) can be found on pages 210–212 and in the Digital Resources. Use the answer keys and rubrics to assess students' work. Be sure to share these rubrics with students so that they know what is expected of them.

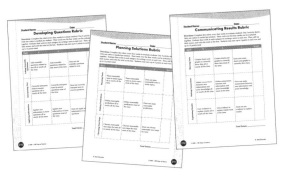

How to Use This Book *(cont.)*

Diagnostic Assessment

Teachers can use the practice pages as diagnostic assessments. The data analysis tools included with the book enable teachers or parents to quickly score students' work and monitor their progress. Teachers and parents can see which skills students may need to target further to develop proficiency.

Students will learn science content, how to analyze data, how to develop scientific questions, how to plan solutions, and how to accurately communicate results. You can assess students' learning using the answer key for all days. Rubrics are also provided on pages 210–212 for Days 3–5 to help you further assess key analytical skills that are needed for success with the scientific practices. Then, record their scores on the Practice Page Item Analysis sheets (pages 213–215). These charts are provided as PDFs, Microsoft Word® files, and Microsoft Excel® files. Teachers can input data into the electronic files directly, or they can print the pages.

To Complete the Practice Page Analysis Charts

- Write or type students' names in the far-left column. Depending on the number of students, more than one copy of the form may be needed or you may need to add rows.
  - The science strands are indicated across the tops of the charts.
  - Students should be assessed every four weeks, as indicated in the first rows of the charts.
- For each student, evaluate his or her work over the past four weeks using the answer key for Days 1 and 2 and the rubrics for Days 3–5.
- Review students' work for the weeks indicated in the chart. For example, if using the *Life Science Analysis Chart* for the first time, review students' work from weeks 1–4. Add the scores for Days 1 and 2 for each student, and record those in the appropriate columns. Then, write students' rubric scores for Days 3–5 in the corresponding columns. Use these scores as benchmarks to determine how each student is performing.

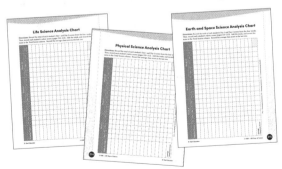

Digital Resources

The Digital Resources contain digital copies of the rubrics, analysis sheets, and standards correlations. See page 216 for more information.

How to Use This Book *(cont.)*

Using the Results to Differentiate Instruction

Once results are gathered and analyzed, teachers can use the results to inform the way they differentiate instruction. The data can help determine which science skills and topics are the most difficult for students and which students need additional instructional support and continued practice.

Whole-Class Support

The results of the diagnostic analysis may show that the entire class is struggling with certain science topics. If these concepts have been taught in the past, this indicates that further instruction or reteaching is necessary. If these concepts have not been taught in the past, this data is a great preassessment and may demonstrate that students do not have a working knowledge of the concepts. Thus, careful planning for the length of the unit(s) or lesson(s) must be considered, and additional front-loading may be required.

Small-Group or Individual Support

The results of the diagnostic analysis may show that an individual student or a small group of students is struggling with certain science skills. If these concepts have been taught in the past, this indicates that further instruction or reteaching is necessary. Consider pulling these students aside to instruct them further on the concepts while others are working independently. Students may also benefit from extra practice using games or computer-based resources.

Teachers can also use the results to help identify proficient individual students or groups of students who are ready for enrichment or above-grade-level instruction. These students may benefit from independent learning contracts or more challenging activities.

Standards Correlations

Shell Education is committed to producing educational materials that are research and standards based. In this effort, we have correlated all of our products to the academic standards of all 50 states, the District of Columbia, the Department of Defense Dependents Schools, and all Canadian provinces.

How to Find Standards Correlations

To print a customized correlation report of this product for your state, visit our website at **www.teachercreatedmaterials.com/administrators/correlations/** and follow the on-screen directions. If you require assistance in printing correlation reports, please contact our Customer Service Department at 1-877-777-3450.

Purpose and Intent of Standards

The Every Student Succeeds Act (ESSA) mandates that all states adopt challenging academic standards that help students meet the goal of college and career readiness. While many states already adopted academic standards prior to ESSA, the act continues to hold states accountable for detailed and comprehensive standards.

Standards are designed to focus instruction and guide adoption of curricula. Standards are statements that describe the criteria necessary for students to meet specific academic goals. They define the knowledge, skills, and content students should acquire at each level. Standards are also used to develop standardized tests to evaluate students' academic progress. Teachers are required to demonstrate how their lessons meet state standards. State standards are used in the development of all of our products, so educators can be assured they meet the academic requirements of each state.

McREL Compendium

Each year, McREL analyzes state standards and revises the compendium to produce a general compilation of national standards. The standards listed on page 10 support the objectives presented throughout the weeks.

Next Generation Science Standards

This set of national standards aims to incorporate knowledge and process standards into a cohesive framework. The standards listed on pages 10–13 support the objectives presented throughout the weeks.

Standards Correlations *(cont.)*

180 Days of Science is designed to give students daily practice in the three strands of science. The weeks support the McREL standards and NGSS performance expectations listed in the charts below.

McREL Standards		
Standard	**Weeks**	**Unit**
Knows different ways in which living things can be grouped and purposes of different groupings.	1, 2	Life Science
Knows that living organisms have distinct structures and body systems that serve specific functions in growth, survival, and reproduction.	5–10	Life Science
Knows that all organisms (including humans) cause changes in their environments, and these changes can be beneficial or detrimental.	11, 12	Life Science
Knows that an object's motion can be described by tracing and measuring its position over time.	1, 2	Physical Science
Knows that heat can move from one object to another by conduction and that some materials conduct heat better than others.	5	Physical Science
Knows that when a force is applied to an object, the object either speeds up, slows down, or goes in a different direction.	6, 7	Physical Science
Knows that light can be reflected, refracted, or absorbed.	12	Physical Science
Knows how features on the Earth's surface are constantly changed by a combination of slow and rapid processes.	1, 4	Earth and Space Science

Next Generation Science Standards					
Unit	**Week**	**Performance Expectation**	**Science and Engineering Practices**	**Disciplinary Core Ideas**	**Cross-Cutting Concepts**
Life Science	1	Construct an argument that plants and animals have internal and external structures that function to support survival, growth, behavior, and reproduction.	Engaging in Argument from Evidence	Structure and Function	Systems and System Models
	2	Construct an argument that plants and animals have internal and external structures that function to support survival, growth, behavior, and reproduction.	Engaging in Argument from Evidence	Structure and Function	Systems and System Models
	3	Construct an argument that plants and animals have internal and external structures that function to support survival, growth, behavior, and reproduction.	Engaging in Argument from Evidence	Structure and Function	Systems and System Models
	4	Construct an argument that plants and animals have internal and external structures that function to support survival, growth, behavior, and reproduction.	Engaging in Argument from Evidence	Structure and Function	Systems and System Models

Standards Correlations *(cont.)*

Unit	Week	Performance Expectation	Science and Engineering Practices	Disciplinary Core Ideas	Cross-Cutting Concepts
Life Science	5	Construct an argument that plants and animals have internal and external structures that function to support survival, growth, behavior, and reproduction.	Engaging in Argument from Evidence	Structure and Function	Systems and System Models
	6	Construct an argument that plants and animals have internal and external structures that function to support survival, growth, behavior, and reproduction.	Engaging in Argument from Evidence	Structure and Function	Systems and System Models
	7	Use a model to describe that animals receive different types of information through their senses, process the information in their brain, and respond to the information in different ways.	Developing and Using Models	Information Processing	Systems and System Models
	8	Use a model to describe that animals receive different types of information through their senses, process the information in their brain, and respond to the information in different ways.	Developing and Using Models	Information Processing	Systems and System Models
	9	Use a model to describe that animals receive different types of information through their senses, process the information in their brain, and respond to the information in different ways.	Developing and Using Models	Information Processing	Systems and System Models
	10	Use a model to describe that animals receive different types of information through their senses, process the information in their brain, and respond to the information in different ways.	Developing and Using Models	Information Processing	Systems and System Models
	11	Use a model to describe that animals receive different types of information through their senses, process the information in their brain, and respond to the information in different ways.	Developing and Using Models	N/A	Systems and System Models
	12	Use a model to describe that animals receive different types of information through their senses, process the information in their brain, and respond to the information in different ways.	Engaging in Argument from Evidence	N/A	Systems and System Models
Physical Science	1	Use evidence to construct an explanation relating the speed of an object to the energy of that object.	Constructing Explanations and Designing Solutions	Definitions of Energy	Energy and Matter
	2	Use evidence to construct an explanation relating the speed of an object to the energy of that object.	Constructing Explanations and Designing Solutions	Definitions of Energy	Energy and Matter

Standards Correlations *(cont.)*

Unit	Week	Performance Expectation	Science and Engineering Practices	Disciplinary Core Ideas	Cross-Cutting Concepts
		Next Generation Science Standards			
Physical Science	3	Make observations to provide evidence that energy can be transferred from place to place by sound, light, heat, and electric currents.	Planning and Carrying Out Investigations	Definitions of Energy Conservation of Energy and Energy Transfer	Energy and Matter
	4	Make observations to provide evidence that energy can be transferred from place to place by sound, light, heat, and electric currents.	Planning and Carrying Out Investigations	Definitions of Energy Conservation of Energy and Energy Transfer	Energy and Matter
	5	Make observations to provide evidence that energy can be transferred from place to place by sound, light, heat, and electric currents.	Planning and Carrying Out Investigations	Definitions of Energy Conservation of Energy and Energy Transfer	Energy and Matter
	6	Ask questions and predict outcomes about the changes in energy that occur when objects collide.	Asking Questions and Defining Problems	Definitions of Energy Conservation of Energy and Energy Transfer	Energy and Matter
	7	Ask questions and predict outcomes about the changes in energy that occur when objects collide.	Asking Questions and Defining Problems	Definitions of Energy Conservation of Energy and Energy Transfer	Energy and Matter
	8	Apply scientific ideas to design, test, and refine a device that converts energy from one form to another.	Constructing Explanations and Designing Solutions	Conservation of Energy and Energy Transfer Energy in Chemical Processes and Everyday Life Defining Engineering Problems	Energy and Matter Influence of Engineering, Technology, and Science on Society and the Natural World Science is a Human Endeavor
	9	Develop a model of waves to describe patterns in terms of amplitude and wavelength and that waves can cause objects to move.	Developing and Using Models Scientific Knowledge is Based on Empirical Evidence	Wave Properties	Patterns
	10	Generate and compare multiple solutions that use patterns to transfer information.	Constructing Explanations and Designing Solutions	Information Technologies and Instrumentation Optimizing the Design Solution	Patterns Interdependence of Science, Engineering, and Technology
	11	Generate and compare multiple solutions that use patterns to transfer information.	Constructing Explanations and Designing Solutions	Information Technologies and Instrumentation Optimizing the Design Solution	Patterns Interdependence of Science, Engineering, and Technology
	12	Develop a model to describe that light reflecting from objects and entering the eye allows objects to be seen.	Developing and Using Models	Electromagnetic Radiation	Cause and Effect

Standards Correlations *(cont.)*

Unit	Week	Performance Expectation	Science and Engineering Practices	Disciplinary Core Ideas	Cross-Cutting Concepts
Earth and Space Science	1	Identify evidence from patterns in rock formations and fossils in rock layers to support an explanation for changes in a landscape over time.	Analyzing and Interpreting Data	The History of Planet Earth	Patterns Scientific Knowledge Assumes an Order and Consistency
	2	Identify evidence from patterns in rock formations to support an explanation for changes in a landscape over time.	Constructing Explanations and Designing Solutions	The History of Planet Earth	Patterns Scientific Knowledge Assumes an Order and Consistency
	3	Identify evidence from patterns in rock formations to support an explanation for changes in a landscape over time.	Constructing Explanations and Designing Solutions	The History of Planet Earth	Patterns Scientific Knowledge Assumes an Order and Consistency
	4	Make observations and/or measurements to provide evidence of the effects of weathering or the rate of erosion by water, ice, wind, or vegetation.	Analyzing and Interpreting Data	The History of Planet Earth	Patterns Scientific Knowledge Assumes an Order and Consistency
	5	Make observations and/or measurements to provide evidence of the effects of weathering or the rate of erosion by water, ice, wind, or vegetation.	Planning and Carrying Our Investigations	Earth Materials and Systems Biogeology	Cause and Effect
	6	Make observations and/or measurements to provide evidence of the effects of weathering or the rate of erosion by water, ice, wind, or vegetation.	Planning and Carrying Our Investigations	Earth Materials and Systems Biogeology	Cause and Effect
	7	Analyze and interpret data from maps to describe patterns of Earth's features.	Analyzing and Interpreting Data	Plate Tectonics and Large-Scale System Interactions	Patterns
	8	Analyze and interpret data from maps to describe patterns of Earth's features.	Analyzing and Interpreting Data	Plate Tectonics and Large-Scale System Interactions	Patterns
	9	Obtain and combine information to describe that energy and fuels are derived from natural sources and their uses affect the environment.	Obtaining, Evaluating, and Communicating Information	Natural Resources	Cause and Effect Influence of Engineering, Technology, and Science
	10	Obtain and combine information to describe that energy and fuels are derived from natural sources and their uses affect the environment.	Obtaining, Evaluating, and Communicating Information	Natural Resources	Cause and Effect Influence of Engineering, Technology, and Science
	11	Generate and compare multiple solutions to reduce the impacts of natural Earth processes on humans.	Constructing Explanations and Designing Solutions	Natural Hazards Designing Solutions to Engineering Problems	Cause and Effect Influence of Engineering, Technology, and Science
	12	Generate and compare multiple solutions to reduce the impacts of natural Earth processes on humans.	Constructing Explanations and Designing Solutions	Natural Hazards Designing Solutions to Engineering Problems	Cause and Effect Influence of Engineering, Technology, and Science

Header: **Next Generation Science Standards**

Name: _____ **Date:** _____

Learning Content

Directions: Read the text, and answer the questions.

Vertebrates and Invertebrates

Some animals have backbones. They are called vertebrates. Birds, fish, and lizards are vertebrates. So are cats and dogs. Humans are vertebrates, too. All vertebrates have skeletons made of bone or cartilage. They also have brains. Their brains are protected by skeletal framework called a skull.

Animals without backbones are invertebrates. Spiders, insects, and worms are invertebrates that live on land. Crabs, jellyfish, and clams are invertebrates that live in water. They either don't have brains or have very simple brains. They do not have bones. Often, they have hard outer coverings. These coverings help protect them.

invertebrate

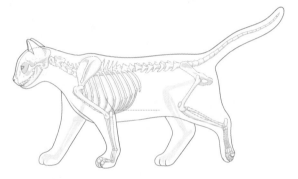

vertebrate

1. Which animal is an invertebrate?

   a. parrot

   b. eagle

   c. giraffe

   d. ladybug

2. All vertebrates _____ .

   a. are warm blooded

   b. have tails

   c. have backbones

   d. have fur or hair

3. Why doesn't an animal's home tell you whether it is a vertebrate or invertebrate?

   _____

   _____

   _____

   _____

Name: _____ **Date:** _____

Directions: Study the chart, and answer the questions.

Vertebrate	Characteristics
mammals	hair or fur, warm-blooded, live births, lungs, live on land
birds	feathers, warm-blooded, lay eggs, lungs, live on land
reptiles	scales, cold-blooded, lay eggs, lungs, live on land and in water
amphibians	smooth skin, cold-blooded, lay eggs, lungs, live on land and in water
fish	scales, cold-blooded, lay eggs, gills, live in water

1. Some vertebrates are warm-blooded, and some are cold-blooded. Which vertebrate is warm-blooded?

   a. fish   **b.** amphibian

   c. bird   **d.** reptile

2. What do fish and reptiles have in common besides backbones?

   a. They live on land.   **b.** They have scales.

   c. They lay eggs.   **d.** both b and c

3. What is one major difference between mammals and other vertebrates?

   _____

   _____

Name: _____ Date: _____

Developing Questions

Directions: Read the text, and answer the questions.

Dylan is a paleontologist. This means that she is a scientist who studies fossils. Fossils are the remains of animals and plants that lived long ago. They can help us learn many things. Dylan finds a new fossil. She wants to know if the animal was a vertebrate or an invertebrate.

1. What part would tell Dylan that the fossil is a vertebrate?

   a. the shell

   b. the backbone

   c. the muscles

   d. the stem

2. What other part would tell Dylan that the fossil is from a vertebrate?

   a. antenna

   b. a heart

   c. a skull

   d. a shell

3. What is a question that Dylan might ask about the fossil to find out what type of animal it was?

   _____

   _____

   _____

4. What is a type of vertebrate that a paleontologist might find?

   _____

Name: _____ Date: _____

Directions: Read the text, and look at the picture of an animal's backbone. Then, answer the questions.

> Animals with backbones tend to be faster and stronger than animals without backbones. One of the functions of a backbone is to help support an animal's weight. A backbone isn't a single bone. It is made up of many small bones. These bones are called vertebrae. Vertebrae make an animal's backbone flexible. They allow an animal to move freely. If the backbone were one solid bone, the animal would be stiff. It couldn't walk or bend over.
>
> Lauren wants to make a model of a backbone for the science fair.

1. What characteristics of a backbone does Lauren need to show in her model for the science fair?

   a. It is strong, but not very flexible.

   b. It is flexible, but not very strong.

   c. It is both strong and flexible.

   d. It is neither strong nor flexible.

2. Which materials would be best for Lauren to use in her model backbone?

   a. a pipe cleaner with beads on it

   b. a string with beads strung on it

   c. a craft stick with beads glued on it

   d. a craft stick without beads

3. How could Lauren demonstrate how a backbone supports an animal's weight but still lets the animal be flexible?

   _____

   _____

   _____

   _____

Life Science

Name: _____ Date: _____

Directions: Study the list of animals. Complete the chart by writing each animal in the correct category.

lion	jellyfish	ant	salmon
eagle	cow	alligator	catfish
snake	raven	salamander	dog
frog	turtle	spider	

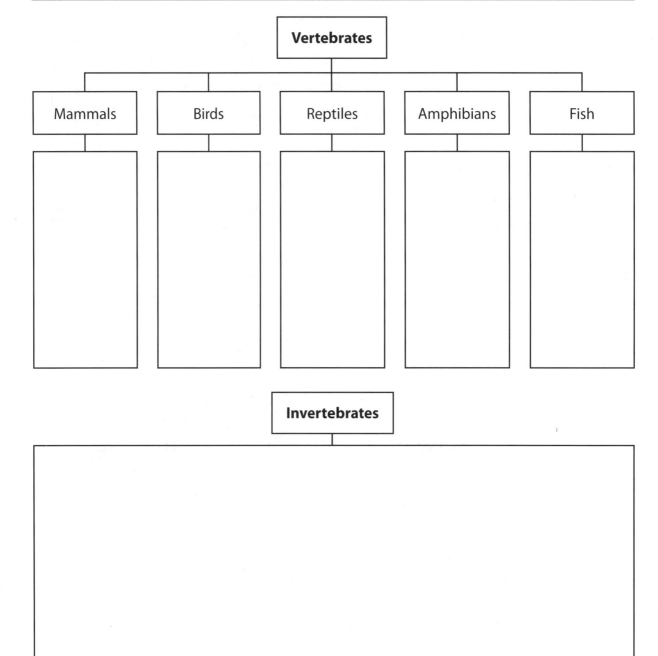

Vertebrates

Mammals	Birds	Reptiles	Amphibians	Fish

Invertebrates

Name: _____ Date: _____

Directions: Read the text, and answer the questions.

Land and Water Animals

Animals live in every kind of habitat on Earth. Some live their entire lives on the land. They cannot live underwater. They are called terrestrial animals. Some live their entire lives in the water. They cannot live out in the air. They are called aquatic animals. All animals are adapted to their habitats. For instance, land animals have legs and feet to help them walk and run. Aquatic animals have fins or flippers to help them swim. Some animals, like frogs and newts, spend part of their lives living in water and part living on land. They are called amphibians.

1. Animals that live on land are called _____ .

    a. mammals   **b.** land-lovers

    c. aquatic animals   **d.** terrestrial animals

2. Most animals who live in the water have _____ .

    a. legs for running   **b.** teeth to catch prey

    c. fins or flippers for swimming   **d.** fur or hair for warmth

3. Name one terrestrial animal you might have as a pet. Name one aquatic animal you might have as a pet.

    _____

    _____

4. What kind of animal is a frog?

    _____

Analyzing Data

Name: _____   Date: _____

Directions: Study the infographic, and answer the questions.

Amphibians

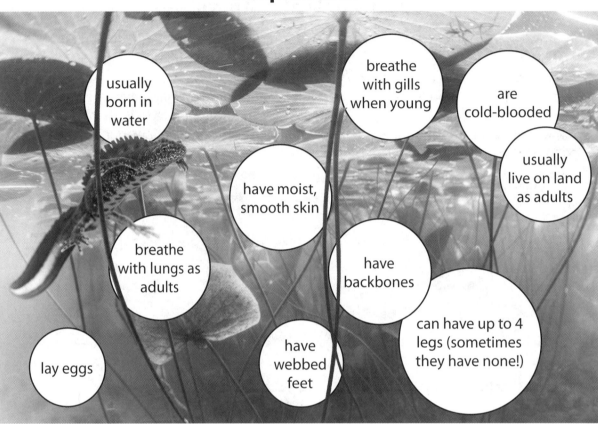

usually born in water

breathe with gills when young

are cold-blooded

usually live on land as adults

have moist, smooth skin

breathe with lungs as adults

have backbones

lay eggs

have webbed feet

can have up to 4 legs (sometimes they have none!)

1. How do amphibians breathe as adults?

   a. with lungs

   b. with gills

   c. with lungs and gills

   d. They don't breathe.

2. Amphibians are _____ .

   a. warm-blooded

   b. cold-blooded

   c. warm-blooded only as adults

   d. cold-blooded only as adults

3. What are the main differences between young amphibians and adult amphibians?

   _____

   _____

   _____

51410—180 Days of Science

Name: _____   Date: _____

Directions: Read the text, and answer the questions.

> Dylan is a paleontologist, which is a scientist who studies fossils. Fossils are the remains of animals that lived long ago.
>
> Dylan found a new fossil. She has decided the fossil came from an animal with a backbone. Now she wants to know if the animal was a land or a water animal. She knows that bones of terrestrial animals tend to be more dense, or solid, than the bones of aquatic animals. She compares the bones of her fossil to the bones of a whale fossil. The bones of her fossil are denser than the bones of the whale fossil.

Developing Questions

1. Why did Dylan compare the bones of her fossil to a whale fossil?

   a. She wanted to see if her fossil's bones were denser than an aquatic animal's.

   b. She needed to compare her fossil to another fossil of the same age.

   c. She needed to compare her fossil to another fossil of the same size.

   d. She already knows that her fossil is a whale, so she wanted to compare with another whale.

2. What does the density of her fossil's bones tell Dylan?

   a. The fossil probably was an aquatic animal.

   b. The fossil probably was an amphibian.

   c. The fossil probably was a terrestrial animal.

   d. The fossil probably was a bird.

3. What is another question that Dylan can ask about the fossil to determine if it was a terrestrial animal?

   _____

   _____

   _____

Name: _____ **Date:** _____

Planning Solutions

Directions: Read the text, and answer the questions.

You are a zookeeper. You get a new baby clownfish for the aquarium. You want the baby clownfish to grow into an adult. You know that clownfish live in the warm, tropical ocean. It is very important that clownfish have water that is warm enough. It's your job to make sure your new fish has everything it needs to be healthy.

1. What is the first thing you need to do before you put the fish in its tank?

   a. Make sure there aren't any other fish in the tank.

   b. Make sure the water is warm enough.

   c. Make sure the fish has something to eat.

   d. Make sure there is enough light in the tank.

2. How can you tell if the clownfish has the right habitat?

   a. It will grow bigger.

   b. It will stay the same size

   c. It will stop swimming.

   d. It will become friends with other fish.

3. How can you determine what kinds of fish can live together in the same tank?

   _____

   _____

   _____

   _____

Name: _____ Date: _____

Directions: Read the text, and study the list of animals. Then, fill out the chart. Put each animal where you might see it.

Animals who spend their lives on land are called terrestrial animals. Animals who spend their lives in water are called aquatic animals. Amphibians live in water when they are young, but they spend most of their time on land as adults.

| frog | deer | jellyfish | newt |
| ant | dolphin | monkey | wolf |

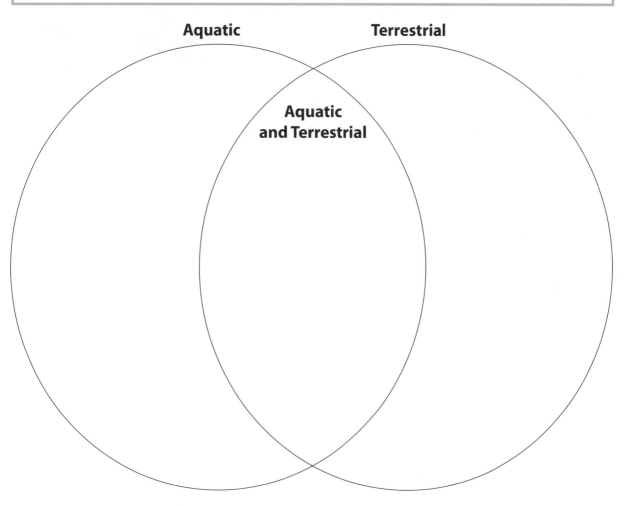

Aquatic　　　　　**Terrestrial**

Aquatic and Terrestrial

1. What is unique about amphibians?

_____

_____

_____

Communicating Results

ABC

Name: _____ Date: _____

Directions: Read the text, and answer the questions.

Plant Structures

Plants are made up of several different structures. The roots of a plant are located under the ground. They help hold the plant up and carry water and nutrients from the soil. The stem can be seen above the ground. It is the central part of a plant. The stem is important because branches and leaves grow from it. Leaves are important because they help plants make food by absorbing sunlight.

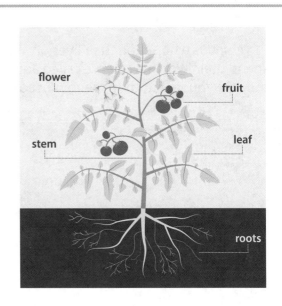

1. Leaves are important to a plant's growth because _____ .

   a. they keep plants from falling over

   b. they help plants make food

   c. they protect plants from bugs

   d. they produce seeds

2. What is the central part of a plant?

   a. roots

   b. leaves

   c. stem

   d. fruit

3. Why are the roots of a plant located underground?

   _____

   _____

   _____

Name: _____ **Date:** _____

Directions: Study the diagram, and answer the questions.

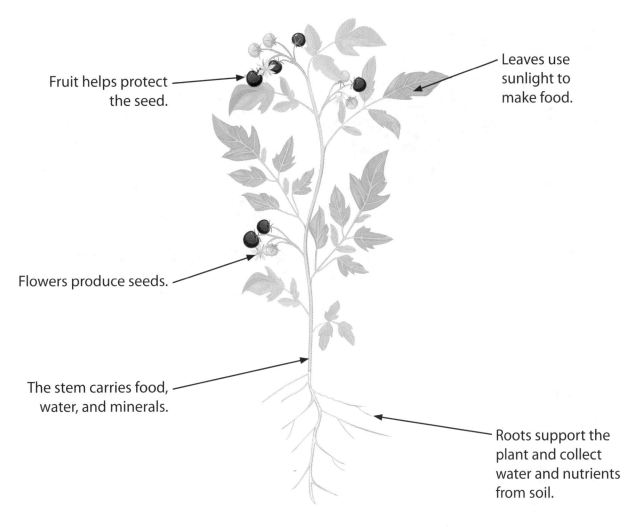

Fruit helps protect the seed.

Leaves use sunlight to make food.

Flowers produce seeds.

The stem carries food, water, and minerals.

Roots support the plant and collect water and nutrients from soil.

Analyzing Data

1. What part of a plant produces the seeds?

  a. leaf

  c. stem

  b. flower

  d. roots

2. What parts of a plant transport water?

  a. stem and leaves

  c. fruit and flowers

  b. leaves and roots

  d. stem and roots

3. What are the main purposes of the roots of a plant?

_____

_____

Name: _____ **Date:** _____

Directions: Read the text. Answer the questions.

Colt is helping his mother in their vegetable garden. She asks him to gather some carrots and onions. When Colt pulls the carrots and onions from the ground, he notices that the onions have small, thin roots on the bottom. The carrot is one big root. The small roots are called fibrous roots. The carrot is a taproot.

1. What part of the carrot plant do people eat?

   a. leaves

   b. root

   c. stem

   d. flowers

2. What does the difference in root structure tell Colt?

   a. The two plants have the same needs.

   b. The two plants have different needs.

   c. The two plants taste the same.

   d. The two plants are related.

3. What is a question Colt might ask about these two different types of roots?

_____

_____

_____

Name: _____ **Date:** _____

Directions: Read the text, and answer the questions.

> Sayo plants two sunflowers. They get the same amount of water. One of the sunflowers is growing tall. The other one is hardly growing. Sayo knows that plants use sunlight to make food in their leaves. He wants to know why the sunflowers aren't growing at the same rate.

Planning Solutions

1. If the sunflowers are getting the same amount of water, what else might affect their growth?

   a. size of the stems

   b. color of the stems

   c. amount of sunlight

   d. number of flowers

2. If one sunflower has brown leaves and the other has green, what might that tell Sayo?

   a. The plant with the green leaves is making enough food to grow.

   b. The plant with the brown leaves isn't making enough food to grow.

   c. The number of leaves doesn't tell Sayo anything important.

   d. both a and b

3. If the sunflowers have the same color leaves, what is an experiment that Sayo could do to find out why the sunflowers aren't growing at the same rate?

   _____

   _____

   _____

4. Could the amount of light that a plant gets affect its growth? Why or why not?

   _____

   _____

   _____

Name: _____ **Date:** _____

Directions: Study the data in the chart. Then, create a graph from the data that shows how long it takes each plant to be ready to harvest.

Plant	Days to Harvest
beets	70 days
carrots	80 days
lettuce	45 days
onions	120 days
peas	80 days
tomatoes	80 days

Time to Harvest Different Plants

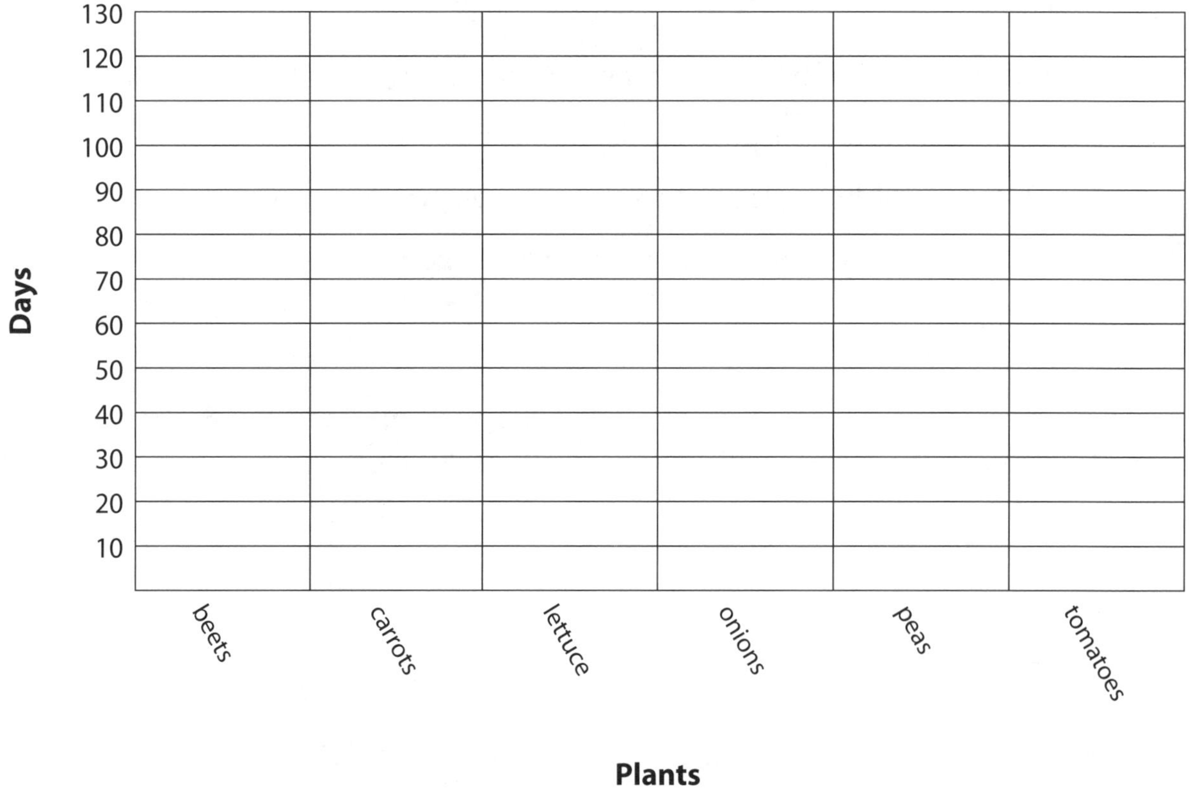

Days

130
120
110
100
90
80
70
60
50
40
30
20
10

beets   carrots   lettuce   onions   peas   tomatoes

Plants

1. We eat young leaves of lettuce, but we eat the mature roots of carrots. Which one do we have to wait longer to eat?

_____

Name: _____ **Date:** _____

Directions: Read the text, and answer the questions.

Nocturnal Animals

Some animals sleep during the day and are awake at night. These animals are called nocturnal. Animals that sleep at night and are awake during the day are called diurnal. Many animals are nocturnal. They eat and are active at night. Often, they are awake at night because it's easier for them to hunt prey in the dark. Even some big hunters like leopards and wolves are nocturnal.

Learning Content

1. A nocturnal animal _____ .

    a. sleeps all night   **b.** sleeps during the day

    c. is always able to fly   **d.** is not very big

2. During the night, nocturnal animals _____ .

    a. hunt   **b.** eat

    c. are active   **d.** all of the above

3. Why might it be easier to hunt prey in the dark?

_____

_____

4. Are people nocturnal or diurnal? Explain your answer.

_____

_____

Name: _____ **Date:** _____

Analyzing Data

Directions: Owls have special body parts that help them hunt at night. Study the diagram, and answer the questions.

large head — big eyes

curved beak

strong wings — thick feathers

sharp talons

1. Which body part is the most helpful in the darkness?

   a. curved beak   **b.** strong wings

   c. big eyes   **d.** thick feathers

2. Nights are colder than days. Which adaptation helps an owl stay warm at night?

   a. big eyes   **b.** thick feathers

   c. sharp talons   **d.** strong wings

3. If you were to create a nocturnal wolf, what features would you include? Why?

   _____

   _____

   _____

   _____

   _____

Developing Questions

Name: _____ Date: _____

Directions: Read the text, and answer the questions.

Cats are nocturnal animals because they prefer to be active at night. Wild cats sleep almost all day. They hunt at night. However, domestic, or pet, cats are often awake at least part of the day. Often, their owners will feed them or play with them during the day. This usually causes them to sleep more at night and less during the day.

1. Why do you think a pet cat might be awake during the day?

   a. They prefer sleeping in the dark.

   b. They are afraid of being left alone.

   c. They want to play with their owners.

   d. They aren't happy with their cat beds.

2. Do you think you can train a cat to sleep all night instead of all day?

   a. No, nocturnal animals will always sleep all day.

   b. Yes, you just have to ask nicely.

   c. No, but they will be awake more of the day if you feed and play with them then.

   d. Yes, but only if they have a dog to play with.

3. What is a question you could ask a veterinarian to learn more about nocturnal animals?

   _____

   _____

   _____

4. Hamsters eat and exercise at night. Are these pets nocturnal? How do you know?

   _____

   _____

   _____

Name: _____ **Date:** _____

Directions: Read the text, and answer the questions.

> A zoo has an area where visitors can see bats. Because bats are nocturnal, it will be hard for zoo visitors to see them. They would normally be asleep when the zoo is open.

1. What is the best way for the zoo to help visitors observe the bats?

    a. There is nothing they an do. Visitors will just have to see sleeping bats.

    b. The zookeepers can make the bat exhibit dark so the bats think it is night.

    c. The zoo can have special bat visiting hours at night.

    d. Either b or c.

2. What is one thing the bats will do when they are awake?

    a. hibernate

    b. search for food

    c. fly

    d. both b and c

3. If you had to test three different ways to help zoo visitors see nocturnal animals during the day, what things might you try?

    _____

    _____

    _____

4. What are some other things nocturnal animals might do at night?

    _____

    _____

    _____

Name: _____ Date: _____

Directions: Animals that are active at night must have senses that help them survive at night. Look at the chart. Write the animals in the correct section of the diagram. Then, answer the questions.

ABC

Communicating Results

	Bat (Nocturnal)	Owl (Nocturnal)	Dog (Diurnal)	Raccoon (Nocturnal)	Cow (Diurnal)
Hearing	excellent	excellent	good	excellent	good
Night vision	fair	excellent	fair	excellent	fair
Sense of smell	excellent	poor	excellent	excellent	good

Nocturnal	Diurnal

1. Which senses are important for nocturnal animals? Why?

   _____

   _____

   _____

2. What do you notice about the senses of diurnal animals?

   _____

   _____

   _____

Learning Content

Name: _____ **Date:** _____

Directions: Read the text, and answer the questions.

How Birds Fly

Birds have bodies that are adapted, or specially designed, to fly. They fly mainly by flapping their wings, but that is not the only thing that helps them fly. Birds have wing feathers that help propel and lift them. They are able to steer with their tail feathers. Their bodies are light and aerodynamic. Aerodynamic means they easily move through the air. Part of why their bodies are so light is how their bones are structured. The main bones in their wings are actually hollow.

1. Why are birds' bodies so light?

    a. Their feet are large.

    b. Some of their bones are hollow.

    c. They have lots of feathers.

    d. Their bones are very dense.

2. What body part do birds use to steer?

    a. beak

    b. body

    c. wings

    d. tail

3. What does *aerodynamic* mean?

    a. Able to move easily through the air.

    b. Able to flap wings quickly.

    c. Able to lift high off the ground.

    d. Able to steer in every direction.

Name: _____ **Date:** _____

Directions: Read the text, and study the pictures. Then, answer the questions.

> Different birds have different types of wings. Each type of wing is ideal for a different type of flying. Some birds, like the albatross and hawk, soar on air currents for long periods of time without flapping their wings much. Other birds, like sparrows and ducks, flap their wings a lot.

Albatross
long soaring wing

Sparrow
curved wing
to quickly change
directions

Duck
high-speed wing

Hummingbird
wings for hovering

Hawk
broad soaring wing

1. Which bird can fly for long periods of time without flapping its wings?

    a. hummingbird   **b.** duck

    c. sparrow   **d.** albatross

2. Which bird can hover in place?

    a. hawk   **b.** duck

    c. hummingbird   **d.** sparrow

3. Which type of bird can quickly change directions?

    a. albatross   **b.** sparrow

    c. hawk   **d.** duck

Developing Questions

Name: _____ Date: _____

Directions: Read the text, and answer the questions.

Birds' feathers are an important part of their ability to fly. If a bird loses too many wing or tail feathers, it can't fly.

Laila sees a bird that is missing feathers from one of its wings. It is hopping around on the ground, and doesn't fly away when she walks toward it. She can see that the bird is not injured.

1. What is a possible reason that the bird doesn't fly away?

    a. It lost too many feathers.

    b. Its legs don't work.

    c. It has too many feathers.

    d. Its beak is too big.

2. Will the bird be able to fly again if its feathers grow back?

    a. Yes, if it is not sick or injured.

    b. Yes, if it grooms itself first.

    c. No, the new feathers would be the wrong color.

    d. No, the new feathers wouldn't work the same as the old ones.

3. What is a question Laila could ask about the bird's wing?

    _____

    _____

4. Do you think the bird would have the same problem if it was missing tail feathers instead of wing feathers? Why or why not?

    _____

    _____

    _____

Name: _____ Date: _____

Directions: Read the text, and study the diagram. Then, answer the questions.

> Jamie is studying the difference between bird wings and human arms. He learns that human bones are dense and heavy, but bird bones are hollow and light. Both wings and arms have similar types of bones. They both bend at joints. Jamie wants to build a model of a bird wing.

Planning Solutions

Arm and Wing Anatomy

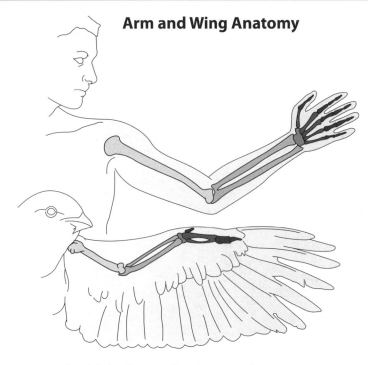

1. What could Jamie use to build the bones for the wing?

   a. straws because they're light and hollow

   b. sticks because they're solid

   c. pipe cleaners because they're flexible

   d. ribbon because it's soft

2. Should the model of the wing be flexible?

   a. Yes, because bird wings bend at joints.

   b. Yes, because bird bones are flexible.

   c. No, because bird wings do not have joints.

   d. No, because bird wings don't move.

3. How can Jamie's model show what's the same and what's different between a wing and an arm?

   _____

   _____

Name: _____ Date: _____

Directions: Read the text, and study the data. Create a graph from the data that shows how fast different flightless birds can travel.

Although all birds have wings, some birds cannot fly at all. These birds are called flightless birds. Some flightless birds are slow-moving, but some can run as fast as a car or swim faster than a person.

Bird	Top Speed in Kilometers Per Hour
ostrich	72
emperor penguin	14
steamer duck	24
cassowary	50
kiwi	19

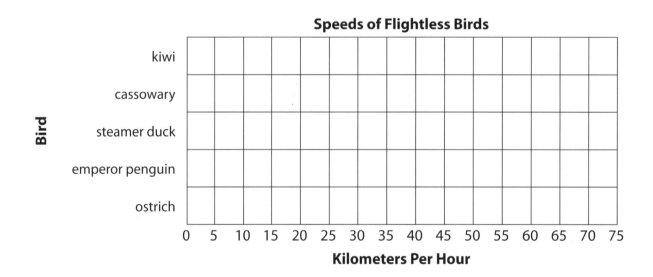

Speeds of Flightless Birds

Bird (y-axis): kiwi, cassowary, steamer duck, emperor penguin, ostrich

Kilometers Per Hour (x-axis): 0 5 10 15 20 25 30 35 40 45 50 55 60 65 70 75

1. Could you run to keep up with an ostrich? Why or why not?

_____

_____

Name: _____ **Date:** _____

Directions: Read the text, and answer the questions.

Different Walks of Life

You may not have given your legs much thought, but do you know how important they are to humans and animals alike? Legs support the body. They let us walk, run, and play sports. They help animals hunt or escape predators. Legs come in pairs. Humans have two. Many animals have four, and insects have six. Legs come in all shapes and sizes, too. Giraffes have very tall, skinny legs. Stick insects have legs that look like branches.

Learning Content

1. How many legs do insects have?

    a. 2   **b.** 4

    c. 6   **d.** 8

2. Why might giraffes have long legs?

    a. To reach leaves in trees.   **b.** To walk over holes in the ground.

    c. To run slowly.   **d.** To dig holes.

3. Why are animals' legs different?

    a. They meet each animal's needs.   **b.** They help animals escape different types of predators.

    c. They help animals get the food they need.   **d.** all of the above

4. People can survive without two legs. Do you think animals can? Why or why not?

_____

_____

_____

Analyzing Data

Name: _____ Date: _____

Directions: Read the text, and study the diagram. Then, answer the questions.

> Human legs consist of the upper leg, which attaches to the hip, the lower leg, and the foot. They are made of many bones, muscles, blood vessels, and nerves. The leg bends at the hip, knee, and ankle. The femur is the longest, largest, and hardest bone in the human body.

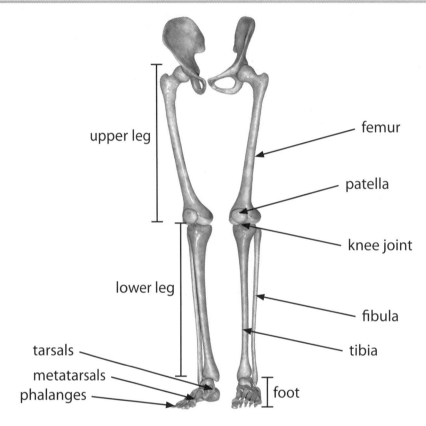

1. Which bone is part of the lower leg?

   a. femur

   b. metatarsals

   c. tibia

   d. phalanges

2. Which bone is the longest?

   a. tibia

   b. femur

   c. fibula

   d. patella

3. Which feature of our legs helps us walk?

   a. flexibility at joints

   b. length of bones

   c. thickness of bones

   d. color of bones

Name: _____ **Date:** _____

Directions: Read the text, and answer the questions.

Developing Questions

> Katie visits the zoo with her father, and they see the giraffes. They have long, graceful necks, but they also have very long, skinny legs. Their legs are 1.8 meters (six feet) long, which is even longer than her dad is tall. Giraffes can also use their legs to defend themselves with powerful kicks. This helps protect them from lions and crocodiles. Katie is amazed that their thin legs can hold up their large bodies. She wonders how this is possible.

1. What can giraffes' legs do?

   a. help them breathe underwater

   b. help them reach food

   c. protect them from lions

   d. both b and c

2. What must giraffe legs be to support their weight?

   a. strong

   b. wide

   c. brown

   d. short

3. What is a question Katie could ask about giraffes' legs?

   _____

   _____

   _____

4. Why do you think a giraffe needs such long legs?

   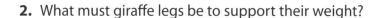

   _____

   _____

   _____

Planning Solutions

Name: _____   Date: _____

Directions: Read the text. Answer the questions.

Rob sometimes sees stick insects. These bugs look like twigs from a tree and have six long, twiggy legs. Their legs and bodies blend in with the environment. Predators often think they're part of a plant. When Rob sees a bird try to grab the bug by a leg, the stick insect detaches its leg and escapes. Rob wants to know how it does this.

1. What do the legs of stick insects look like?

   a. bones

   b. human legs

   c. twigs

   d. furry

2. What's one thing that stick insects use their legs for?

   a. escaping predators

   b. standing out

   c. swimming

   d. digging holes

3. Make a plan for Rob to learn more about the legs of stick insects.

   _____

   _____

   _____

   _____

51410—180 Days of Science

Name: _____ **Date:** _____

Directions: Read the text. Write three things that each type of leg can help its owner do.

> Legs help us do so many things. From work, to play, to survival, legs support us throughout our whole lives.

Communicating Results

ABC

Human

_____

_____

_____

Giraffe

_____

_____

_____

Stick Insect

_____

_____

_____

Learning Content

Name: _____ Date: _____

Directions: Read the text, and answer the questions.

How Do Fish Breathe Underwater?

You may be surprised to know that fish breathe oxygen just like people do. People breathe in, and their lungs take oxygen from the air. Then they breathe out carbon dioxide. Fish don't have lungs, though. They cannot breathe air. They use special organs called gills to absorb oxygen from the water. They also use their gills to release carbon dioxide out of their bodies.

1. What organ do fish use to breathe?

   a. lungs

   b. gills

   c. hearts

   d. scales

2. Would fish be able to get oxygen from air with their gills?

   a. Yes, fish can breathe air or water.

   b. Yes, if they keep their mouths shut.

   c. No, fish can only breathe in water.

   d. No, fish would need legs to breathe air.

3. What do fish get from the water?

   a. carbon dioxide

   b. helium

   c. oxygen

   d. carbon monoxide

Name: _____ Date: _____

Directions: Read the text, and study the diagram. Answer the questions.

Fish cannot breathe air because they don't have lungs. Instead, they use gills to get oxygen from water. Fish pull water into their mouths and push it out their gills. Fish gills have feathery filaments on the inside and gill flaps on the outside. The filaments have many blood vessels that absorb the oxygen. The oxygen is moved into the blood stream. At the same time, the waste carbon dioxide leaves the body through the gills.

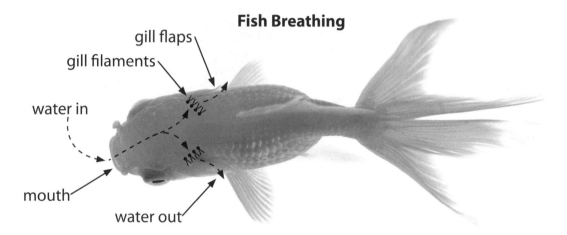

Fish Breathing

gill flaps
gill filaments
water in
mouth
water out

Analyzing Data

1. Which part of the fish absorbs oxygen?

   a. gill flap

   b. gill filaments

   c. mouth

   d. lungs

2. How does water enter the fish?

   a. gills

   b. tail

   c. eyes

   d. mouth

3. Why can't fish breathe air?

   _____

   _____

   _____

Name: _____ **Date:** _____

Developing Questions

Directions: Read the text, and answer the questions.

Abby visits the aquarium where there are many types of fish. She sees clown fish, catfish, stingrays, and sharks. Abby notices that all of the fish, big and small, have gills and are moving their mouths. Even the sharks and stingrays have gills and are moving their mouths. Fish can only breathe underwater. They can't breathe air. Abby wonders what would happen if a fish was not in the water.

1. Do all fish breathe the same way?

    a. Yes, they all use lungs.

    b. Yes, they all use gills.

    c. No, some use gills and other use lungs.

    d. No, some use lungs and other use fins.

2. When she looks at the fish, will they be moving their mouths?

    a. Yes, because they pull in water through their mouths.

    b. Yes, because that's how they communicate.

    c. No, they don't need to open their mouths to breathe.

    d. No, they can pull water in without opening their mouths.

3. What is a question Abby could ask about fish and air?

    _____

    _____

4. Do you think that most fish have gills? Why or why not?

    _____

    _____

Planning Solutions

Name: _____ **Date:** _____

Directions: Read the text, and answer the questions.

Yohan goes to the pet store to buy a fish tank. He chooses a three-gallon tank, and he wants to get as many fish as possible. The pet store employee tells him that he can only have one fish for every gallon of water. Otherwise, there would not be enough oxygen for the fish.

1. Yohan wants to get five fish. What should he do?

   a. Get a larger tank.

   b. Get a different shape tank.

   c. Get two tanks.

   d. either a or c

2. Why is there a limit to the number of fish in a tank?

   a. There is a limited amount of carbon dioxide.

   b. There is a limited amount of oxygen.

   c. There is a limited amount of food.

   d. There is a limited amount of shelter.

3. How can Yohan find out more about keeping fish healthy in a fish tank?

   _____

   _____

4. Do you think the type of fish that Yohan gets could affect how many fish can live in the tank? Why or why not?

   _____

   _____

Communicating Results

Name: _____ Date: _____

Directions: Label the diagram using words from the word bank. Answer the question.

| gill filaments | mouth | gill flaps | water out |

Fish Breathing

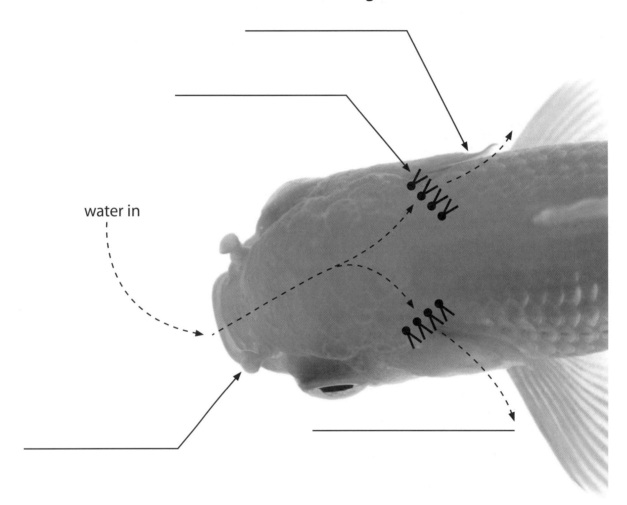

water in

1. What do you think would happen to a fish if it was left out of the water? Explain your answer.

_____

_____

_____

_____

Name: _____ Date: _____

Directions: Read the text, and answer the questions.

Sight

Animals use their senses to interact with the world. The sense of sight is very important. It helps many animals find food and avoid predators. It even helps them find a mate.

The eye is made up of many parts that work together. They send signals to the brain that are decoded so that the animal knows what it is seeing.

Animals all have different sight, which means that the world can look very different to them. Some see more colors than we do, and some see fewer. Some have sharper vision than humans. Some even have more than two eyes. Every animal has eyes that are tailored to their needs.

Learning Content

1. For which action does an animal need sight?

   a. running from predators

   b. hearing other animals

   c. feeling vibrations

   d. tasting new foods

2. Does the world look the same to humans and animals?

   a. Yes, all eyes work the same way.

   b. Yes, all eyes look the same.

   c. No, some eyes see differently.

   d. No, some eyes are used for hearing.

3. Without eyes, what would be difficult for a dog?

   a. playing fetch

   b. finding its bed

   c. finding the front door

   d. all of the above

Name: _____ Date: _____

Directions: Read the text and study the diagram. Answer the questions.

> The eye has many parts that work together. The iris opens and closes to let in light through the pupil. The retina converts light into electrical signals. These signals travel to the brain through the optic nerve. Then the brain tells the animal what it's seeing.

Analyzing Data

Eye

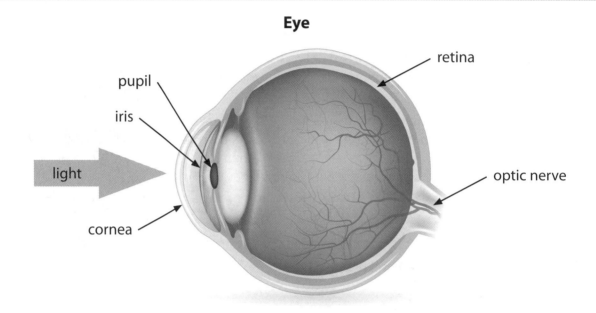

1. Which part of the eye converts light into electrical signals?

   a. pupil   **b.** retina

   c. optic nerve   **d.** iris

2. Which part of the eye opens and closes to let light in through the pupil?

   a. iris   **b.** retina

   c. optic nerve   **d.** cornea

3. Would the eye be able to see without any light at all?

   a. Yes, the eye doesn't need light   **b.** No, very bright light is always
       to see.   needed to see.

   c. Yes, it can see some things   **d.** No, at least some light is needed
       without light.   to see.

Name: _____   Date: _____

Directions: Read the text, and answer the questions.

Kim sometimes sees racoons outside at night. Racoons are nocturnal, which means that they are active at night. Nocturnal animals have eyes that are extra sensitive to light. Their eyes are much better at picking up light than humans' eyes are. Kim wants to know how racoons see at night.

Developing Questions

1. Why can't humans see well in the dark?

   a. Too much light enters humans' eyes.

   b. Humans' eyes are not sensitive enough.

   c. Humans' eyes are the wrong color to see in the dark.

   d. Humans can see very well in the dark.

2. How can nocturnal animals see with less light?

   a. Their eyes are extra sensitive

   b. Their noses are extra sensitive.

   c. Their brains are extra sensitive.

   d. Their paws are extra sensitive.

3. What can Kim ask about racoon eyes?

   _____

   _____

   _____

4. What are some other nocturnal animals you can think of? Do you think their eyes are more sensitive, too?

   _____

   _____

Planning Solutions

Name: _____ **Date:** _____

Directions: Read the text, and answer the questions.

Emily's mom is a dog trainer. She teaches Emily that dogs do not see all the same colors that people do. They see fewer colors. When she trains dogs, she wears clothes that contrast with her environment. The contrasting clothing will help her stand out and be easily seen. This helps make sure that the dogs see her cues. If the colors she wears blend in with the environment, the dog will not easily see her cues and may get confused.

1. How do dogs see colors compared to people?

   a. They see fewer colors.

   b. They see the same colors.

   c. They see more colors.

   d. They see in black and white.

2. Why does Emily's mom wear contrasting clothes?

   a. To stand out.

   b. To blend in.

   c. To be stylish.

   d. To be comfortable.

3. How can Emily use the information about dog eyesight when choosing toys for her dog?

   _____

   _____

   _____

   _____

Name: _____ Date: _____

Directions: Label the diagram using words from the word bank. Answer the questions.

retina (back of the eye)

cornea (covers the iris and pupil)

pupil (lets light in)

iris (opens to let in more light or closes to let in less)

optic nerve (sends signals to the brain)

Eye

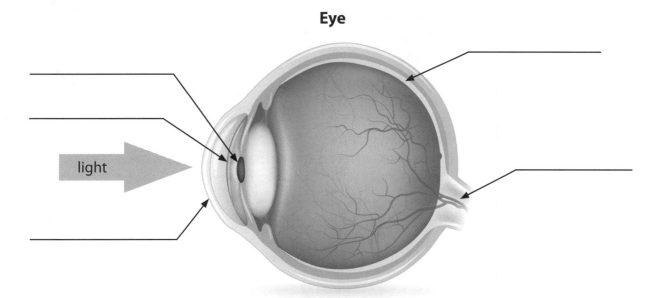

light

1. Where does light enter the eye?

_____

2. The iris opens more when the light is dim. Why is this?

_____

_____

_____

3. What purpose do you think the cornea serves? Explain your answer.

_____

_____

_____

Communicating Results

Name: _____ Date: _____

Learning Content

Directions: Read the text, and answer the questions.

Smell

Smell is very important to animals. It helps them find food or a mate. It also helps them avoid predators. Many animals have a much better sense of smell than people. For example, a dog's sense of smell is about 1,000 times better than a person's.

The inside of the nose is where the body picks up smells. Some animals, like snakes and crabs, have other organs that help them smell. Snakes have something called a Jacobson's organ in their mouth that detects scents that their tongues catch. Crabs have hairs near their mouth that "smell" what's in the water.

1. Do all animals use noses to smell?

    a. Yes, all animals have noses like humans.

    b. Yes, but all animals have noses that look different.

    c. No, some animals have other organs that are used to smell.

    d. No, the sense of smell is not important to animals.

2. Which animal uses its tongue to pick up smells?

    a. snake

    b. crab

    c. bird

    d. human

3. How much stronger is a dog's sense of smell than a human's?

    a. 10 times

    b. 100 times

    c. 1,000 times

    d. 10,000 times

4. What do you think would happen if a dog lost its sense of smell? Why?

_____

_____

Name: _____ Date: _____

Analyzing Data

Directions: Read the text, and study the picture. Then, answer the questions.

Most animals smell by breathing in through the nose. The inside of the nose picks up scents. Then the brain processes signals from the inside of the nose. Dogs and some other animals also have a special organ that picks up pheromones. These are scent messages from other animals.

How Dogs Smell

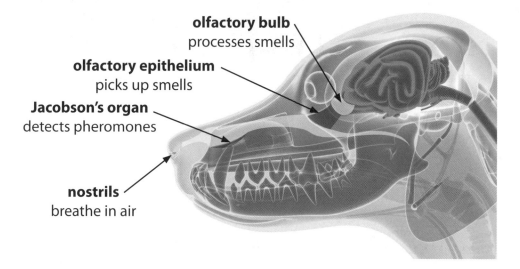

olfactory bulb
processes smells

olfactory epithelium
picks up smells

Jacobson's organ
detects pheromones

nostrils
breathe in air

1. Which organ processes smells?

   a. olfactory bulb   **b.** olfactory epithelium

   c. nostrils   **d.** Jacobson's organ

2. Which body part picks up messages from other animals?

   a. olfactory epithelium   **b.** Jacobson's organ

   c. nostrils   **d.** olfactory bulb

3. Which body part picks up smells?

   a. olfactory bulb   **b.** olfactory epithelium

   c. nostrils   **d.** Jacobson's organ

4. Where is the olfactory bulb located?

   a. in the brain   **b.** in the mouth

   c. in the throat   **d.** in the ear

Name: _____ **Date:** _____

Developing Questions

Directions: Read the text, and answer the questions.

> Snakes have a special organ that they use to detect scents. It is called Jacobson's organ. It is inside their mouth.
>
> Luis has a pet snake. It is always flicking its tongue in the air. He is not sure why the snake does this.

1. Why does the snake flick its tongue in the air?

   a. To pick up smells.

   b. To catch flies.

   c. To make sound.

   d. To hear.

2. How is the snake's tongue involved in smelling?

   a. It brings scents to the Jacobson's organ.

   b. It brings tastes to the Jacobson's organ.

   c. It brings scents to the brain.

   d. It brings scents to the nose.

3. What can Luis ask about the snake's sense of smell?

   _____

   _____

   _____

4. Do you think snakes can smell things that people can't? Why or why not?

   _____

   _____

   _____

Name: _____   Date: _____

Directions: Read the text, and answer the questions.

Sadaf has a dog who loves peanut butter. She gets her dog three special toys that can hold treats. You can't see the treat inside. She fills one with peanut butter, one with a baby carrot, and one with an apple slice. When she gives her dog the treats, the dog smells the toys and quickly finds the one with peanut butter.

Planning Solutions

1. How could Sadaf make it harder for the dog to use smell to find the toy with peanut butter?

   a. Use toys that are see-through.

   b. Hide the toys in different places.

   c. Put the toys right in front of the dog.

   d. Put the peanut butter in a bowl.

2. Sadaf can't smell anything on her hands, but her dog keeps smelling her hand after she makes the treats. Why might this be?

   a. The dog has a stronger sense of smell and can smell food.

   b. The dog does not have a very good sense of smell.

   c. The dog is trying to figure out who she is.

   d. Sadaf's hands don't smell like anything.

3. What is another way that Sadaf can test her dog's sense of smell?

   _____

   _____

   _____

   _____

Name: _____   Date: _____

Directions: Sadaf researched common jobs that different breeds of dogs do in her area. Look at the chart, and fill out the graph.

Dog	Type of Work
Bassett Hound	hunting
Beagle	law enforcement
Belgian Malinois	military
Black and Tan Coonhound	hunting
Bloodhound	law enforcement
Bluetick Coonhound	hunting
Dachshund	hunting
German Shepherd	law enforcement
Golden Retriever	search and rescue
Labrador Retriever	search and rescue

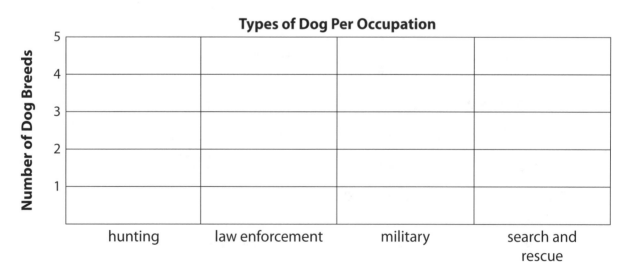

Types of Dog Per Occupation

Number of Dog Breeds

hunting   law enforcement   military   search and rescue

Occupation

1. Which type of job is most common for dogs in this area? Which type is least common?

_____

_____

Name: _____ Date: _____

Directions: Read the text, and answer the questions.

Hearing

To hear something, an animal's ears must first pick up sound waves. The sound waves are converted to signals in the inner ear that are sent to the brain. Then, the brain interprets the signals as sounds.

The ear is responsible for hearing, and it also helps with balance. Part of the inner ear contains fluid and sensors that detect the movement of the head. This helps the brain know how the body is positioned.

Many animals can hear sounds that humans cannot. For example, a dog's ears can hear much higher pitched sounds than a human's ears. Animals use their hearing to find food, find a mate, and avoid predators. Some animals, like bats, even listen to echoes to understand their surroundings.

1. Bats can listen to _____ to understand their surroundings.

   a. echoes

   b. chirps

   c. barks

   d. whispers

2. Which part of the body interprets the signals created by the ear?

   a. nose

   b. eye

   c. brain

   d. heart

3. What can dogs hear that humans cannot?

   a. loud sounds

   b. very high-pitched sounds

   c. music

   d. talking

Name: _____ **Date:** _____

Analyzing Data

Directions: Read the text, and study the picture. Then, answer the questions.

> Animals hear when sound waves travel into the outer ear. The sound waves cause the ear drum to vibrate. Then the vibrations travel through parts of the middle and inner ear. The auditory nerve carries signals to the brain. Then the brain interprets these signals as sounds we recognize.

Cat Ear

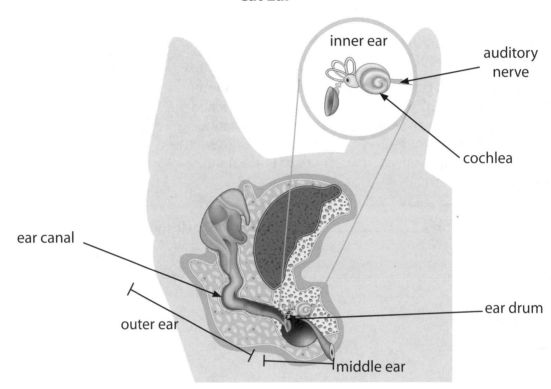

1. Where does sound enter the ear?

   a. inner ear

   c. middle ear

   b. outer ear

   d. auditory nerve

2. Which part sends signals to the brain?

   a. auditory nerve

   c. cochlea

   b. ear canal

   d. ear drum

3. In which part of the ear is the ear canal?

   a. inner ear

   c. middle ear

   b. outer ear

   d. ear drum

Name: _____ Date: _____

Directions: Read the text, and answer the questions.

> The ears are not only responsible for hearing. They are responsible for balance as well.
>
> Jett has a cat named Mika. Mika has been rubbing her ear with her paw a lot. She isn't responding to her name unless he says it loud, and she seems less balanced than normal.

Developing Questions

1. With which body part might Mika have a problem?

    a. paw

    b. tongue

    c. ear

    d. eye

2. If Mika has a problem with her ear, what might it affect?

    a. hearing and balance

    b. balance and sight

    c. balance and taste

    d. hearing and sight

3. What can Jett ask about Mika's balance?

    _____

    _____

    _____

4. What could Jett do to find out what is wrong with Mika?

    _____

    _____

    _____

Planning Solutions

Name: _____ **Date:** _____

Directions: Read the text, and answer the questions.

> April is playing with her dog outside. Her dog stops and turns one ear to the side. He seems to be listening to something that April can't hear. A few moments later, April hears sirens in the distance.

1. What is April's dog probably hearing when he turns his ear?

   a. a cat

   b. sirens

   c. cars

   d. any of these

2. If April's dog hears the sirens before April, what does this mean?

   a. He can hear closer sounds.

   b. He can hear more distant sounds.

   c. He can hear sirens, and April can't.

   d. He can't hear sirens.

3. April gets a dog whistle. Dog whistles are so high-pitched that humans can't hear them, but dogs can. How can she use the whistle to test her dog's hearing?

   _____

   _____

4. Have you ever been able to hear something that someone else could not? Explain why you think this is.

   _____

   _____

   _____

Name: _____ Date: _____

Directions: Label the diagram with words from the word bank. Answer the questions.

inner ear (contains cochlea)	auditory nerve (connected to cochlea)
outer ear (where sound enters)	ear canal (a long tube in the outer ear)
ear drum (in the middle ear)	

Cat Ear

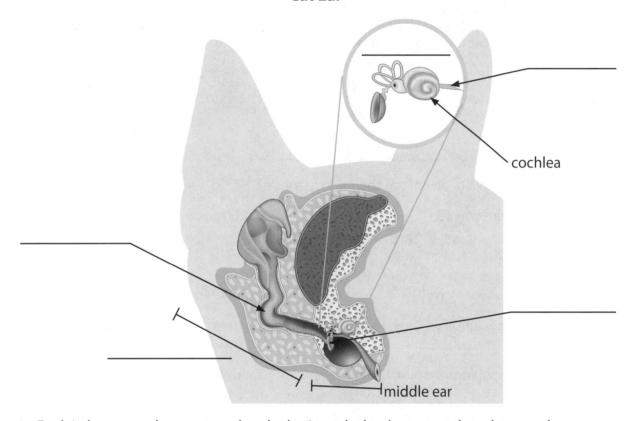

cochlea

middle ear

1. Explain how sound waves travel to the brain and what happens when they get there.

_____

_____

_____

2. Do you think humans' ears work similarly to dogs'? Why or why not?

_____

_____

_____

Communicating Results

ABC

Learning Content

Name: _____ **Date:** _____

Directions: Read the text. Answer the questions.

How Animals Change Their World

Every animal does things to change the world. Some changes are small, like a squirrel burying an acorn. Some changes are big, like a beaver building a dam. All of these changes affect the ecosystem. Sometimes the changes are good, like when squirrels bury acorns that grow into trees. Sometimes they're not good, like when animals eat too many plants in an area. Some changes mean that there will be too few or too many of one type of animal. This can hurt the plants and animals in an area.

1. What is an example of an animal changing its world?

   a. Burying an acorn.

   c. Eating grass.

   b. Building a dam.

   d. all of the above

2. If there were too many wolves in an area, how might this affect the deer?

   a. The deer population would become too large.

   c. The deer population wouldn't change.

   b. The deer population would become too small.

   d. The deer population would double.

3. If a disease killed all the wolves, what would happen to the deer population?

   _____

   _____

4. What are some other ways that animals change the world?

   _____

   _____

   _____

Name: _____ **Date:** _____

Directions: Animals change the world in many ways. Study the chart, and answer the questions.

Animal	Change It Makes	Affect on the World
squirrel	buries acorns	new trees grow
beaver	builds dams	creates new pond ecosystems
woodpecker	makes holes in trees	creates nest sites for other animals
gopher	digs tunnels underground	improves soil quality

Analyzing Data

1. Which animal plants new trees?

   a. woodpecker   **b.** beaver

   c. squirrel   **d.** gopher

2. If gophers moved out of an area, what could happen to the plants?

   a. They would stop growing.   **b.** They might not get all the nutrients they need.

   c. Their soil would improve.   **d.** Nothing would change.

3. What could happen if woodpeckers stopped making holes in trees?

   _____

   _____

   _____

Developing Questions

Name: _____ **Date:** _____

Directions: Read the text, and answer the questions.

Cathy's grandparents live near a forest. She has always seen lots of deer in the forest. This year, the deer are gone. Cathy's grandpa said that the deer had become overpopulated, and they ate all their favorite plants. The plants couldn't grow back fast enough, so the deer left to find food somewhere else.

1. What could have caused the deer to become overpopulated?

   a. The wolves in the area became overpopulated.

   b. There was not enough food for the deer.

   c. Disease killed most of the wolves in the area.

   d. Disease killed some of the deer.

2. Why couldn't the plants grow back fast enough?

   a. There were too many deer eating them.

   b. There was plenty of rain.

   c. The soil was bad.

   d. There was plenty of sun.

3. What can Cathy ask about deer overpopulation?

   _____

   _____

   _____

   _____

Planning Solutions

Name: _____ Date: _____

Directions: Read the text, and answer the questions.

> Jacob and his brother find a beaver dam in a nearby river. The dam is made of logs, sticks, and mud. The beaver used trees from the nearby forest to build its dam. The dam changed the flow of the river and created a new pond. Jacob notices that there are many animals living in the new pond that he does not see in the river. He wonders what would happen if the beaver's dam was removed.

1. What is one way the beaver dam did *not* affect the environment?

   a. Created a new ecosystem.

   b. Changed the flow of the river.

   c. Removed trees.

   d. Planted trees.

2. How did the beaver affect the homes of other animals?

   a. It created new homes.

   b. It took away homes.

   c. It created and took away homes.

   d. It did not affect other animals' homes.

3. How can Jacob learn more about the way the beaver's dam affects the ecosystem?

   _____

   _____

   _____

   _____

Communicating Results

Name: ______________________ Date: ______________

Directions: Kim finds a beaver dam across a river that created a new pond. Draw a picture of the beaver dam and pond. Draw animals that might live in the new pond habitat. Then, answer the question.

1. Explain your picture.

____

____

____

Name: _____   Date: _____

Directions: Read the text. Answer the questions.

How Humans Change Our World

Humans make huge changes to the world. Think about the way a city looks compared to the way a forest looks. A forest is full of trees, other plants, and animals. A city is full of buildings, cars, and concrete. There is no doubt that we are able to change the environment to meet our needs. The changes humans make can have a positive or negative effect. We have to make efforts to take care of the ecosystems that surround us.

Learning Content

1. What is an example of humans changing the world?

   a. tornado

   b. hurricane

   c. polluted water

   d. tsunami

2. What is an example of a positive change that people can make to the world?

   a. Cutting down trees in a forest.

   b. Catching too many fish in a lake.

   c. Planting trees in a park.

   d. Dumping chemicals in the ocean.

3. If humans build a city, how could it affect the plants and animals in the area?

   _____

   _____

   _____

Analyzing Data

Name: _____ Date: _____

Directions: Read the text, and study the chart. Then, answer the questions.

Humans change the world in many ways. Changes can be both good and bad. Many changes help humans and hurt the environment at the same time.

Change	How it Affects the World
cut down trees for wood	provides building materials, removes animal homes
plant trees	provides a home and food for birds and other animals
build farms	provides food for people, pollutes water with fertilizer
build factories	provides products for many people, pollutes the air
recycle	reduces garbage in landfills, reduces pollution

1. What is something humans can do that doesn't hurt the environment?

   a. plant trees

   b. cut down trees for wood

   c. build farms

   d. build factories

2. Which human action contributes to air pollution?

   a. building farms

   b. building factories

   c. recycling

   d. planting trees

3. Which human action reduces garbage in landfills?

   a. building factories

   b. recycling

   c. cutting down trees

   d. building farms

Name: _____ Date: _____

Directions: Read the text, and answer the questions.

Many trees in Reggie's town were cut down to build a new shopping mall. The town organized a day for everyone to come plant trees in a park. Reggie and his family plant a tree together.

1. What change did people make that could hurt the world?

a. planted trees

b. cut down trees

c. went shopping

d. played at a park

2. What was the benefit of planting trees at the park?

a. They will provide new homes for animals.

b. They will provide shade when they grow.

c. They will be beautiful.

d. all of the above

3. What is a question Reggie can ask about the trees they planted?

_____

_____

_____

4. What is another way that Reggie can help the environment?

_____

_____

Planning Solutions

Name: _____ Date: _____

Directions: Read the text, and answer the questions.

Jenna learns that every time she throws something away, it goes into a landfill. Landfills are areas where trash is buried. It is buried in a way that keeps it from coming into contact with the groundwater and air. This means it breaks down very slowly. Jenna wants to start recycling to put less trash in the landfill.

1. How will recycling help the environment?

   a. It creates less waste.

   b. It creates more waste.

   c. It creates more air pollution.

   d. It creates more water pollution.

2. Why is it a problem if trash in landfills breaks down slowly?

   a. It will take up too much space.

   b. It won't take up enough space.

   c. It gives animals a place to play.

   d. It is not a problem.

3. What are some other things Jenna can do to help the environment?

   _____

   _____

   _____

   _____

Name: _____ **Date:** _____

Directions: Draw a picture of two ways you affect the world. Then, answer the question.

1. Why is it important that humans try to take good care of the environment?

_____

_____

_____

Learning Content

Name: _____ Date: _____

Directions: Read the text, and answer the questions.

Speed and Energy

Energy is the ability to do work. There are two main types of energy. There is the energy of motion, which is called kinetic energy. There is also stored energy, which is called potential energy. A ball sitting on top of a hill has a lot of stored energy. The stored energy will change to movement when the ball rolls down the hill. The faster the ball rolls, the more kinetic energy it has.

1. What is energy?

   a. The ability to be still.   **b.** The ability to do work.

   c. a ball   **d.** a hill

2. If something is moving fast, what does it have a lot of?

   a. potential energy   **b.** kinetic energy

   c. thermal energy   **d.** chemical energy

3. If a ball is placed up high, what kind of energy does it have?

   a. kinetic   **b.** potential

   c. chemical   **d.** thermal

4. If a ball is sitting on top of a hill, when will its potential energy change to kinetic energy?

   a. when it rolls down the hill   **b.** when it stops rolling

   c. when it changes colors   **d.** when it changes temperature

5. If one ball is rolling slowly and another ball is rolling quickly, which one has more kinetic energy? How do you know?

   _____

   _____

Analyzing Data

Name: _____ Date: _____

Directions: Read the text, and study the chart. Then, answer the questions.

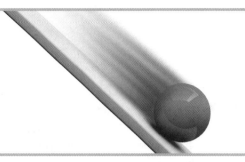

If you roll a ball down a one-meter ramp, the height of the ramp affects the energy of the ball. The faster the ball rolls, the more energy it has.

Height of Ramp (cm)	Speed of Ball (meters per second)	Time to Reach the Bottom (s)
3	0.61	1.65
6	0.8	1.25
9	1.03	0.97
12	1.28	0.78

1. At which height will the ball have the most energy?

   a. 3 cm   **b.** 12 cm

   c. 9 cm   **d.** 6 cm

2. At which height will the ball have the least energy?

   a. 3 cm   **b.** 12 cm

   c. 9 cm   **d.** 6 cm

3. When the ball has more energy, what is happening?

   a. The ball is rolling faster.   **b.** The ball is rolling slower.

   c. The ball is rolling at the same speed.   **d.** It is stopped.

4. What is the connection between the speed of the ball and the time to reach the bottom of the ramp?

   _____

   _____

Developing Questions

Name: _____   **Date:** _____

Directions: Read the text, and answer the questions.

Beth is building a track for marbles. The marble will start high up and then roll up and down over hills. She wants the marble to travel all the way to the end. She builds small hills on her first try. She tests the track, and the marble reaches the end.

1. How was the marble able to reach the end?

   a. It had enough energy from rolling down the track.

   b. It did not have enough energy.

   c. Beth put it at the end.

   d. The marble made its own energy.

2. If the marble started from the ground instead of up high, would it have rolled up the hills? How do you know?

   _____

   _____

   _____

3. What is a question Beth can ask about the height of the hills in her roller coaster?

   _____

   _____

   _____

4. When the marble sits at the top of the roller coaster, does it have potential or kinetic energy?

   _____

Name: _____ **Date:** _____

Directions: Read the text, and look at the picture. Then, answer the questions.

Beth is building a track for marbles. The marble will start high up and then roll up and down over hills. She wants the marble to travel all the way to the end. On her first try, she built hills lower than the starting point. On her second try, she builds a hill that is higher than the starting point. The marble won't go over the first hill. It will only go over a hill that is lower than the starting point.

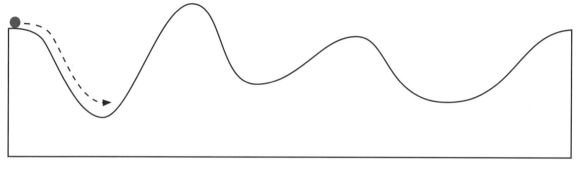

1. Why can't the marble go over the hill?

   a. It has enough energy.

   b. It doesn't have enough energy.

   c. The hill is too low.

   d. The marble is red.

2. What's the highest the marble can climb?

   a. just shorter than the starting point

   b. twice as high as the starting point

   c. just higher than the starting point

   d. three times as high as the starting point

3. How can Beth change her track so that the marble will get over the hill?

   _____

   _____

   _____

   _____

Planning Solutions

Name: _____ **Date:** _____

Directions: Read the text, and draw a marble track. Then, answer the question.

> If a marble rolls down a track, it can go up hills. But, the hills cannot be higher than where the marble started.

Communicating Results

ABC

1. Explain why you drew your marble track the way you did.

_____

_____

_____

Name: _____ Date: _____

Directions: Read the text, and answer the questions.

Fast and Furious

Energy is the ability to do work. Energy can't be created or destroyed. It can be changed or transferred between objects.

Have you ever played with a wind-up car? When you pull it back and let go, it moves forward. The car has a spring inside that winds up tight when you pull the car back. The spring has stored energy, or potential energy. When you let it go, the spring unwinds and transfers its energy to the wheels. The potential energy changes to kinetic energy, or movement. How far it goes depends on how far you pull it back.

1. What is kinetic energy?

   a. movement

   c. heat

   b. stillness

   d. radiation

2. What is potential energy?

   a. movement

   c. radiation

   b. stored energy

   d. heat

3. What can happen to energy?

   a. It can be created.

   c. It can be transferred.

   b. It can be destroyed.

   d. none of the above

4. How can you get the car to go as far as possible?

   _____

   _____

   _____

Learning Content

Analyzing Data

Name: _____ Date: _____

Directions: Read the text. Study the chart. Answer the questions.

Marcy built a rubber band car. She used CDs for the wheels and a wooden skewer to connect the wheels. She used cardboard for the body of the car and a rubber band to power it. When she wraps the rubber band around the axle, it pulls tighter and has more potential energy.

Number of Times Rubber Band is Wound	Total Distance	Total Time
1	6 cm	1 second
3	12 cm	2 seconds
6	18 cm	3 seconds
9	24 cm	4 seconds

1. If she winds the rubber band more, what happens to the car?

   a. It doesn't go as far.   **b.** It goes farther.

   c. It goes the same distance.   **d.** It doesn't move.

2. When she lets the car go, what kind of energy does it have?

   a. potential   **b.** thermal

   c. chemical   **d.** kinetic

3. If Marcy wants the car to go as far as possible, what should she do?

   a. Not wind the rubber band.   **b.** Wind the rubber band as many times as she can.

   c. Wind the rubber band three times. **d.** Wind the rubber band twice.

Name: _____ **Date:** _____

Directions: Read the text, and answer the questions.

Nick and his friend Wes want to race their toy cars. They have two of the same cars. They make a starting line and a finish line on the carpet. They push their cars gently, and they don't roll very fast. Neither car reaches the finish line. They measure the distance that the cars traveled, and they each traveled 1.2 meters (4 feet).

1. Which type of energy do the cars need more of to reach the finish line?

   a. kinetic

   b. thermal

   c. sound

   d. chemical

2. What would happen if they pushed the cars harder?

   a. They would travel less than 1.2 meters.

   b. They would travel more than 1.2 meters.

   c. They would not move.

   d. They would travel 1 meters.

3. What is a question Nick can ask about how far the cars travel?

   _____

   _____

   _____

4. Do you think the type of floor affects how far the cars go? Why or why not?

   _____

   _____

Planning Solutions

Name: _____ **Date:** _____

Directions: Read the text, and answer the questions.

Nick and his friend Wes are racing toy cars. They have two of the same cars. First, they push their cars gently on carpet, and they only roll 1.2 meters (4 feet). This time they push their cars on the carpet, but they push much harder. They roll 2.4 meters (8 feet).

1. Why did the cars go farther the second time?

   a. The harder push gave them more energy.

   b. The harder push gave them less energy.

   c. The type of floor changed.

   d. The type of car changed.

2. If Nick pushed his car harder than Wes, who's car would go farther?

   a. Wes's

   b. Nick's

   c. They would go the same distance.

   d. There is no way of knowing.

3. What could Nick change about his experiment to get the cars to roll as far as possible?

   _____

   _____

   _____

4. If Nick and Wes used different cars, would this affect the experiment? Why or why not?

   _____

   _____

Name: _____ **Date:** _____

Directions: The chart shows the distance traveled by a rubber band car. Graph the data, and answer the questions.

Number of Times Rubber Band is Wound	Total Distance
1	6 cm
3	12 cm
6	18 cm
9	24 cm
12	35 cm

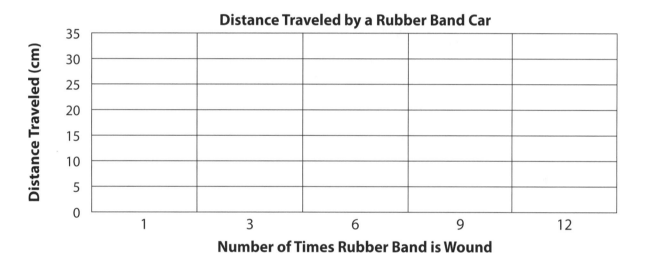

1. What other variables could affect the distance traveled by the car?

_____

_____

_____

2. Would a ramp affect the car?

_____

_____

_____

Communicating Results

Learning Content

Name: _____   **Date:** _____

Directions: Read the text, and answer the questions.

Why Do Light Bulbs Get Hot?

Energy can't be created or destroyed. It can only change or move between objects. A light bulb is a good example of how electrical energy changes to light and heat. Light and heat are both types of energy. Some light bulbs are made of a glass bulb with a piece of wire inside, called a filament. When one of these light bulbs is turned on, electricity flows through the filament. It then heats up until it is bright enough to make light.

1. What is a filament?

   a. wire

   b. glass

   c. electricity

   d. heat

2. Which is not a type of energy?

   a. electricity

   b. light

   c. heat

   d. glass

3. Electrical energy changes into _____ and _____ in a light bulb.

   a. light and sound

   b. heat and sound

   c. light and heat

   d. sound and electricty

Name: _____ **Date:** _____

Directions: Read the text, and study the diagram. Then, answer the questions.

When you use a light bulb, electrical energy enters the filament. The filament heats up and creates light. The purpose of the light bulb is light, so the heat energy is wasted.

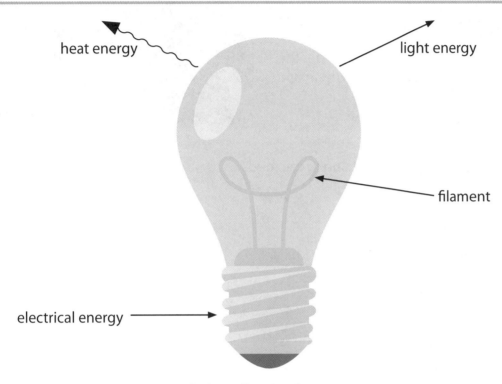

heat energy

light energy

filament

electrical energy

1. When the electricity enters the light bulb, what happens?

   a. The filament would create dim light.   **b.** The filament would create bright light.

   c. The filament would not create light.   **d.** The filament would break.

2. If there was no electrical energy, what would happen?

   a. The filament would create dim light.   **b.** The filament would create bright light.

   c. The filament would not create light.   **d.** The filament would break.

3. Which object would use the heat from a light bulb?

   a. floor lamp in an office   **b.** flash light at a campsite

   c. food warming lamp at a restaurant   **d.** refrigerator lamp in an office

Name: _____ Date: _____

Directions: Read the text, and answer the questions.

> Wes goes to a restaurant with his family, and they sit near the kitchen. He sees that the cooks set plates of food under lights called heat lamps. The plates sit under the heat lamps until the servers pick them up.

Developing Questions

1. What are the lights probably doing to the food?

   a. Cooling it off.

   b. Keeping it warm.

   c. Showing the waiters where it is.

   d. Making it look delicious.

2. Is the heat energy from the lights being wasted?

   a. Yes, there is no use for the heat.

   b. Yes, the heat is only warming the air around the lamp.

   c. No, the heat is keeping the food warm.

   d. No, the heat is keeping the cooks warm.

3. What might Wes ask about the food sitting under the lights?

   _____

   _____

4. What is the benefit of heat lamps in restaurants?

   _____

   _____

   _____

Name: _____ **Date:** _____

Directions: Read the text, and answer the questions.

Lindsey goes to the pet store to pick out a pet. She chooses a lizard. The pet store clerk tells her that she has to use a heat lamp to provide the lizard with light and heat.

Planning Solutions

1. Which types of energy are created by a heat lamp?

   a. heat

   b. light

   c. chemical

   d. both a and b

2. What is another way Lindsey could give her lizard light and heat energy?

   a. Put the cage in the sunlight.

   b. Put the cage in the closet.

   c. Put the cage in the basement.

   d. Put the cage in a shadow.

3. How can Lindsey test what kind of heat lamp is the best for her lizard?

   _____

   _____

   _____

4. What are some other ways that Lindsey could use the heat from a light bulb?

   _____

   _____

Name: _____ **Date:** _____

Communicating Results

Directions: Label the diagram using words from the bank. Then, answer the questions.

| filament | electrical energy | light energy | heat energy |

1. Explain how energy is transferred in an electric light bulb.

   _____

   _____

   _____

2. If a light bulb is off, how can you tell that it has been recently used?

   _____

   _____

   _____

3. List three objects in which a light bulb would be used.

   _____

Learning Content

Name: _____   Date: _____

Directions: Read the text, and answer the questions.

The Sound of Energy

Electricity is a type of energy. It can be changed into sound. Speakers use electricity to make sound. They have a metal coil inside called an electromagnet. It vibrates when electricity runs through it. The vibrations pass through a cone. The cone amplifies the vibrations and pushes them into the air. Sound travels through the air to reach our ears.

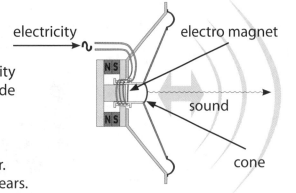

electricity

electro magnet

sound

cone

1. When you listen to headphones, what kind of energy changes into sound?

    a. heat

    b. chemical

    c. electricity

    d. kinetic

2. Which part of the speaker makes the vibrations?

    a. cone

    b. plug

    c. electromagnet

    d. case

3. Which part of the speaker amplifies the sound waves?

    a. cone

    b. electromagnet

    c. power cord

    d. case

4. Do you think you could see the vibrations on a speaker? Why or why not?

    _____

    _____

5. Do you think you could hear the sound if the cone did not amplify the vibrations? Why or why not?

    _____

    _____

Name: _____ **Date:** _____

Directions: Read the text, and study the diagram of a speaker. Then, answer the questions.

> When electricity enters a speaker, it vibrates a coil. The vibrations create sound waves that are amplified, or made louder, by the speaker.

Analyzing Data

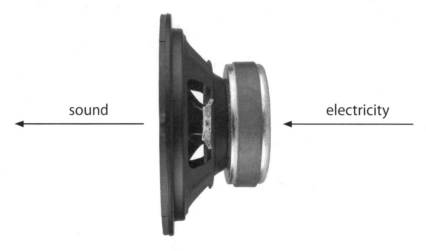

sound ←   ← electricity

1. How is the electric energy transferred to sound energy?

   a. The coil creates electricity.

   b. The hum of electricity creates music.

   c. The electricity causes a coil to vibrate, which creates sounds.

   d. The electricity heats the coil, which creates sounds.

2. What creates sound waves?

   a. heat

   b. vibrations

   c. electricity

   d. power cords

3. How does a speaker help us hear sound waves?

   a. It amplifies them.

   b. It makes them quiet.

   c. It cancels them out.

   d. It uses heat to create them.

Name: _____ Date: _____

Directions: Read the text, and answer the questions.

Deepak gets a pair of wireless headphones for his birthday. After he listens to them for a while, the battery dies. He can't hear his music anymore. The battery is where the electricity comes from. Deepak has to plug in the headphones to charge the battery.

Developing Questions

1. Why can't he hear the music through the headphones when the battery dies?

    a. The battery stores the music.

    b. They need electricity to create sound waves.

    c. They need sound waves to create electricity.

    d. They need heat to create sound waves.

2. If Deepak charges his headphones, what will happen?

    a. The headphones will no longer have electricity.

    b. The headphones will have electricity to work again.

    c. The headphones will have electricity but won't work.

    d. The battery in the headphones cannot be charged.

3. What can Deepak ask about the headphones?

    _____

    _____

    _____

4. List some other things you can think of that convert electricity into sound.

    _____

    _____

    _____

Name: _____ **Date:** _____

Directions: Read the text, and answer the questions.

Deepak's dad has a stereo that has large speakers. When music is playing, he can see the front of the speakers moving back and forth. Movement is kinetic energy. When he turns the volume down, the speakers move less. If he turns off the music, the speakers stop moving.

1. What would happen if Deepak turned the speakers very loud?

   a. They would move less.

   b. They would move more.

   c. They would stop moving.

   d. They would move a different direction.

2. The kinetic energy in the speaker is transfered into _____ energy.

   a. sound

   b. heat

   c. electric

   d. light

3. How can Deepak learn to build a speaker?

   _____

   _____

   _____

4. What do you think would happen if the speaker was unable to move?

   _____

   _____

   _____

Name: _____ **Date:** _____

Directions: Sort the items into the correct categories. Then, answer the questions.

headphones	tambourine	radio	animals
flute	speakers	trumpet	television

Uses Electricity to Make Sound	Does Not Use Electricity to Make Sound

1. All sound is vibrations. What creates the vibrations in a speaker?

_____

_____

_____

2. What devices do you have that use electricity to make sound?

_____

_____

_____

Communicating Results

ABC

Name: _____ Date: _____

Directions: Read the text, and answer the questions.

How Does a Hairdryer Dry Hair?

When you use a hairdryer, electricity is changed into heat and movement. The energy of movement is called kinetic energy. The electricity makes the heating element, which is a coil of wire, heat up. It also powers a fan. The fan spins and blows air over the heating element. The spinning fan also creates sound energy. The air heats up and is pushed out of the hair dryer and onto your hair. The heat and air movement cause water in your hair to evaporate.

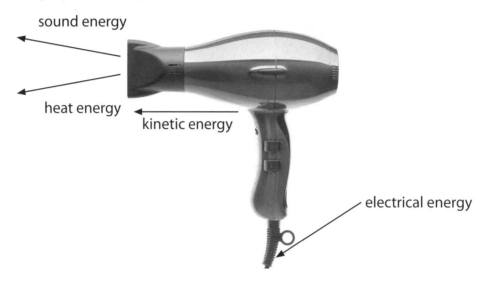

sound energy

heat energy

kinetic energy

electrical energy

---

1. Into which two types of energy does a hair dryer change electricity?

    a. heat and electricity

    b. heat and kinetic

    c. kinetic and chemical

    d. kinetic and potential

2. How does the air become hot?

    a. It blows over the heating element.

    b. The electricity heats the air.

    c. The movement of the air makes it hot.

    d. Fire heats it.

3. If the coil of wire didn't heat up, would the air be hot?

    a. Yes, the movement of the air would heat it.

    b. No, the fan would cool it off.

    c. Yes, a small fire would heat it.

    d. No, the wire is what heats the air.

Name: _____   Date: _____

Directions: Study the diagram, and answer the questions.

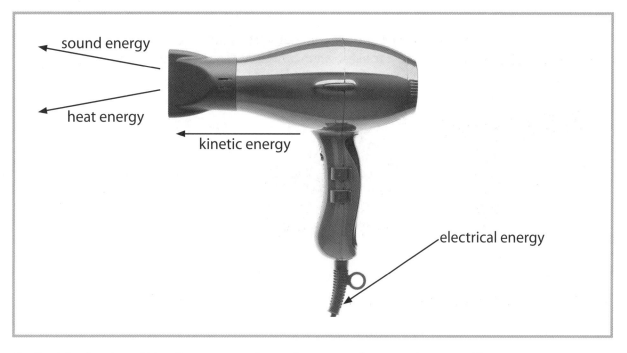

sound energy

heat energy

kinetic energy

electrical energy

Analyzing Data

1. Besides heat and kinetic energy, what other type of energy is created?

   a. sound   **b.** chemical

   c. potential   **d.** magnetic

2. Why won't a hair dryer work if it is not plugged in?

   a. It needs electrical energy to work.   **b.** It needs sound energy to work.

   c. It needs chemical energy to work.   **d.** It needs a longer cord to work.

3. How does a hair dryer dry hair?

   _____

   _____

   _____

4. What are some other items that convert electricity into thermal (heat) energy?

   _____

   _____

   _____

Developing Questions

Name: _____ Date: _____

Directions: Read the text, and answer the questions.

Julie is exploring objects in her house that convert electrical energy to other types of energy. She has a hair dryer, a toaster, an incandescent light bulb, and a pair of headphones.

1. Which object does not convert electrical energy to heat?

   a. toaster

   c. headphones

   b. light bulb

   d. hair dyer

2. Do all of the objects that create heat use the heat in the same way?

   a. Yes, they're all used to make food.

   c. No, they're all used for different things.

   b. Yes, they're all used to dry hair.

   d. No, two are used for the same thing, and one is used for something different.

3. What can Julie ask about converting electrical energy to heat?

   _____

   _____

   _____

4. Besides a toaster, what else can you think of that converts electrical energy to heat to cook food?

   _____

   _____

   _____

Name: _____ **Date:** _____

Directions: Read the text, and answer the questions.

> It is winter, and Julie is cold. She needs something that will help keep her warm. She has a fan, a space heater, and a blanket.
>
>

Planning Solutions

1. Which item uses electrical energy to create thermal (heat) energy?

   a. blanket

   c. fan

   b. space heater

   d. none of them

2. The space heater blows warm air. Which type of energy is the electricity converted to besides heat?

   a. kinetic

   c. light

   b. chemical

   d. electrical

3. Make a plan for Julie to investigate things that use electricity to create heat.

   _____

   _____

   _____

4. If Julie rubs her hands together they get warm. What type of energy is she converting to heat? Explain your answer.

   _____

   _____

   _____

Name: _____ Date: _____

Directions: Read the text, and study the chart. Create a graph that shows how long different hair dryers take to dry hair. Then, answer the questions.

Communicating Results

ABC

Julie borrows hair dryers from her friends. They each put out different amounts of heat. She tries them all to see which dries her hair the fastest.

Hair Dryer	How Long it Takes to Dry Hair
A	12 minutes
B	10 minutes
C	9 minutes
D	13 minutes

Time to Dry Hair

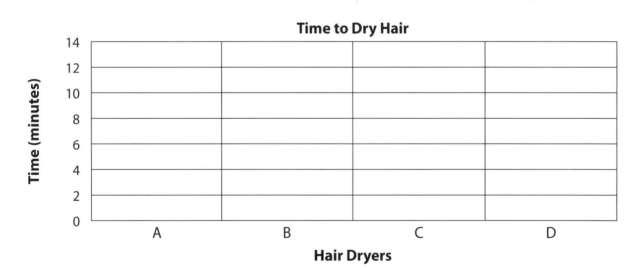

1. Which hair dryer puts out the most heat? How do you know?

_____

_____

_____

Name: _____ **Date:** _____

Directions: Read the text, and answer the questions.

Collision Speed

Crash! Bang! When two things collide, the results can be remarkable. This is all because of energy. Energy is transferred when two things collide.

The moving object passes kinetic energy to the other object. This is the energy of moving objects. Some energy may also be transferred to the air as sound or heat. This is why a bowling ball knocking down pins is so loud. The faster something is moving, the more energy it will transfer.

1. The faster something is moving, the _____ it will transfer.

    a. less energy

    b. less sound

    c. more objects

    d. more energy

2. Which kinds of energy may be released into the air?

    a. heat and sound

    b. sound and potential

    c. sound and kinetic

    d. heat and kinetic

3. When you're bowling, to what does kinetic energy from the ball transfer?

    a. floor

    b. your hand

    c. pins

    d. shoes

4. You roll a bowling ball slowly at pins, and then you roll one faster. What would be the difference in reaction? How do you know?

    _____

    _____

    _____

    _____

Analyzing Data

Name: _____ **Date:** _____

Directions: Read the text, and study the pictures. Then, answer the questions.

> When one object hits another, the energy is transferred. Newton's Cradle can be used to show this. The higher you pull the first ball, the faster it goes. The ball at the other end will swing to almost the same height.

Newton's Cradle

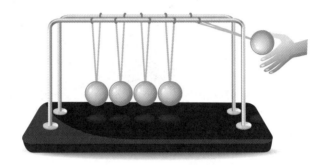

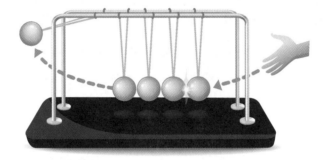

1. If you only lift the first ball a little bit, how high will the last ball swing?

    a. lower

    b. higher

    c. almost the same height

    d. It won't swing.

2. How much of the movement is being transferred?

    a. most of it

    b. some of it

    c. none of it

    d. half of it

3. When you pull the ball higher, it swings faster. How does this affect the transfer of energy?

_____

_____

_____

Name: _____ **Date:** _____

Directions: Marcy rolls a marble down a ruler and hits a cup. It pushes the cup. Study the picture, and answer the questions.

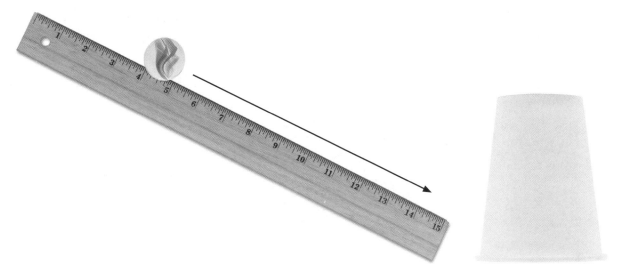

1. Why does the marble push the cup?

   a. It transfers kinetic energy to the cup.

   b. It transfers potential energy to the cup.

   c. It transfers sound to the cup.

   d. It transfers electricity to the cup.

2. If Marcy starts the marble higher on the ruler, how will the cup move?

   a. not as far

   b. farther

   c. the same distance

   d. the opposite direction

3. What is a question Marcy could ask about the ruler and the marble?

   _____

   _____

   _____

Planning Solutions

Name: _____ Date: _____

Directions: Read the text, and answer the questions.

Marcy rolls a marble down a ruler and hits a cup. It pushes the cup. Marcy wants to know how she can push the cup farther.

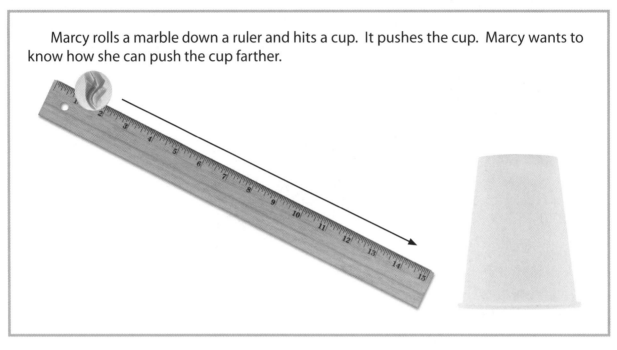

1. How can Marcy change the speed of the marble?

   a. Change its placement on the ruler.   **b.** Change the height of the ruler.

   c. Change the placement of the cup.   **d.** any of these

2. If Marcy replaces the cup with a heavier cup, how could the results of the experiment change?

   a. The cup would move a little farther.   **b.** The cup wouldn't move as far.

   c. The cup would move twice as far.   **d.** The cup would move toward the marble.

3. Plan an experiment to figure out how far Marcy can push the cup.

   _____

   _____

   _____

   _____

Name: _____ **Date:** _____

Directions: Read the text, and study the chart. Create a graph that shows how far the cup can move.

Marcy creates an experiment to see how far she can move a cup by a rolling marble. She places the marble at different heights on a ramp she makes from a ruler.

Position on Ruler	Distance Cup Moved
8 cm	5 cm
15 cm	10 cm
23 cm	15 cm
30 cm	20 cm

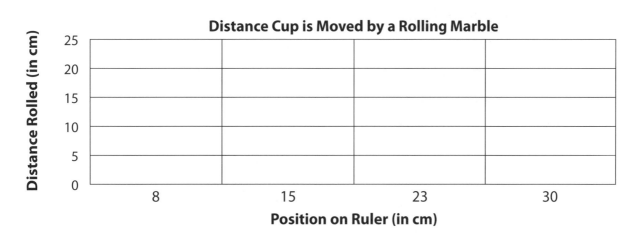

Distance Cup is Moved by a Rolling Marble

Distance Rolled (in cm)

25
20
15
10
5
0

8   15   23   30

Position on Ruler (in cm)

Communicating Results

Name: _____ Date: _____

Learning Content

Directions: Read the text, and answer the questions.

Going in Different Directions

When two things collide, what happens? It depends! Energy is always transferred. Most of the energy is transferred in the form of movement, or kinetic energy. Some is transferred to the air as sound or heat. Sometimes a collision causes an object to speed up. Sometimes it causes an object to slow down. It can even cause an object to change directions.

The speed and weight of the objects affect what happens. If you roll a tennis ball into a wall, it will bounce back. This is because the tennis ball cannot move the wall. If you crash a bowling ball and tennis ball into each other, the bowling ball will make the tennis ball change directions. This is because the bowling ball weighs more than the tennis ball.

1. What can happen when objects collide?

    a. They speed up.   **b.** They slow down.

    c. They change directions.   **d.** all of the above

2. What causes the changes when objects collide?

    a. energy transfer   **b.** bowling balls

    c. tennis balls   **d.** bouncing

3. Which properties of the objects affect what happens?

    a. speed and size   **b.** speed and weight

    c. weight and color   **d.** weight and temperature

4. If a bowling ball and tennis ball collide, what happens? Why?

    _____

    _____

Name: _____   Date: _____

Directions: The red ball and blue ball have the same weight. Study the pictures, and answer the questions.

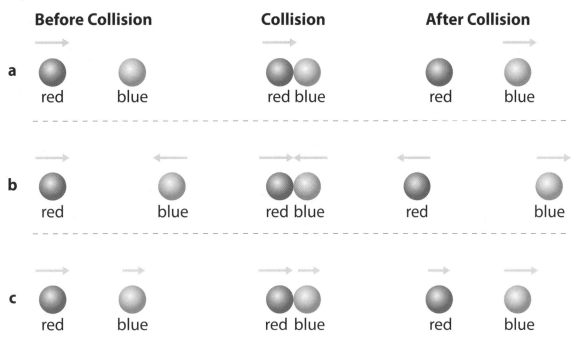

1. When both balls move toward each other, what happens after they collide?

   a. The red ball stops.   **b.** The blue ball stops.

   c. Both balls change directions.   **d.** Both balls move the same way.

2. When both balls move the same direction and collide, what happens?

   a. They keep moving the same direction.   **b.** The red ball stops.

   c. The blue ball stops.   **d.** The blue ball changes directions.

3. If the balls have different weights, would the results be the same? Why or why not?

_____

_____

4. Describe what happens when a moving ball collides with an unmoving ball.

_____

_____

_____

Developing Questions

Name: _____ **Date:** _____

Directions: Read the text, and answer the questions.

Marcus and Nancy build identical ramps for toy cars. They place the ramps opposite each other. They want to roll the cars down the ramps and crash them into each other to see what happens. Nancy chooses a heavy car, and Marcus chooses a light car.

1. How should they build their ramps to make sure they're rolling their cars the same way?

   a. different heights

   b. different lengths

   c. the same height and length

   d. the same color

2. Whose car do you think will change direction during the collision. Why?

   _____

   _____

   _____

   _____

3. What is a question Marcy could ask about the importance of the size of the cars?

   _____

   _____

   _____

Name: _____ Date: _____

Directions: Read the text, and answer the questions.

> Marcus and Nancy build identical ramps for toy cars. They want to crash the cars into each other to see what happens. When they used one heavy car and one light car, the light car changed directions. They want to test other scenarios.
>
>

1. If they use two identical cars, what will happen?

   a. Neither car will change direction.

   b. Marcus's car will change direction.

   c. Nancy's car will change direction.

   d. They will both change direction.

2. If they use two identical cars, and make one ramp higher, will it change the results? Why?

   _____

   _____

3. How can Marcus and Nancy test different scenarios?

   _____

   _____

   _____

   _____

Name: _____ Date: _____

Directions: Draw two balls. Label their weights and the direction they are traveling. Then, answer the questions.

Communicating Results

1. Explain what will happen when the balls collide and why.

_____

_____

_____

2. What would happen if you changed the weight of one of the balls?

_____

_____

_____

Name: _____ **Date:** _____

Directions: Read the text, and answer the questions.

What Kind of Light Bulbs Are the Most Energy-Efficient?

More than 150 years ago, scientists began creating the light bulb. It wasn't just one scientist who created it. Many different scientists worked to make previous ideas better. The incandescent bulb was the first light bulb. They use heat to make light. They also waste a lot of energy.

The original light bulb has been improved many times. Shortages in energy led people to make light bulbs better. Compact fluorescent lights use about 75 percent less energy than incandescent bulbs. They also last about 10 times longer. Now we have LED bulbs. They cut energy use by more than 80 percent They can also last more than 25 times longer than incandescent bulbs. They often cost a lot more than other light bulbs.

incandescent bulb

fluorescent bulb

LED bulb

1. Why would people want to improve light bulbs if there is an energy shortage?

a. to use more energy

b. to use less energy

c. to make brighter lights

d. to make warmer lights

2. If you have a light bulb in a hard-to-reach place, which type of bulb would be the best choice?

a. LED because you don't have to change them as often.

b. Incandescent because you have to change them frequently.

c. Fluorescent because of their compact size.

d. LED because they are very bright.

3. What is a reason that someone might choose an incandescent light bulb instead of an LED light bulb?

_____

_____

Analyzing Data

Name: _____ **Date:** _____

Directions: Read the text, and study the chart. Then, answer the questions.

> Watts are how much power a bulb uses. Lumens are how much light they give off. Lumens per watt measures efficiency. The higher it is, the better.

	Incandescent	Fluorescent	Halogen	CFL	LED
Lumens	850	2,600	1,200	800	800
Watts	60	40	50	13	9.5
Lumens per Watt	14	65	24	62	84
Cost to Operate for 25,000 Hours	$177.50	$112.50	$168.75	$51.38	$36.13

1. Which bulb is the most efficient?

   a. fluorescent

   c. LED

   b. CFL

   d. incandescent

2. Which bulb is the least efficient?

   a. LED

   c. fluorescent

   b. incandescent

   d. CFL

3. Which bulb costs the least to operate?

   a. incandescent

   c. CFL

   b. fluorescent

   d. LED

Name: _____ **Date:** _____

Developing Questions

Directions: Read the text, and look at the chart. Then, answer the questions.

Jeff has an incandescent bulb, a CFL (fluorescent) bulb, and an LED bulb. He needs to put one in a guest room that is rarely used. One needs to go in a living room lamp that is used for several hours every night. One needs to go in an office that is used for an hour each day.

Bulb	Hours of Life	Price
incandescent	1,000	$2
CFL	10,000	$3
LED	25,000	$4

1. Which light bulb should Jeff use for the living room?

    a. CFL because it has the longest life.

    b. LED because it has the longest life.

    c. Incandescent because it is the brightest.

    d. Incandescent because it has the shortest life.

2. Why would it make sense to put the incandescent bulb in the guest room?

    a. The light won't have to be changed often since the room is rarely used.

    b. The room is dark, and it is the brightest bulb.

    c. It will help keep the room cold.

    d. It is the most expensive bulb, and guests might break it.

3. What question should Tom ask his mom about choosing light bulbs?

    _____

    _____

    _____

Name: _____ **Date:** _____

Planning Solutions

Directions: Read the text, and answer the questions.

Tom's mom asked him to buy some light bulbs. He needs five light bulbs, and he has $15.

Incandescent bulbs are $2 each. They are the least efficient. CFL bulbs are $3 each. They are more efficient. LED bulbs are $4 each, and they are the most efficient.

1. What are the most efficient light bulbs that Tom can afford to buy five of?

   a. CFL   b. LED

   c. incandescent   d. none of them

2. Tom's mom doesn't want any incandescent bulbs. What should he buy?

   a. 4 LED and 1 CFL   b. 3 CFL, 1 LED, and 1 incandescent

   c. 5 CFL   d. 5 LED

3. Tom wants to buy the most efficient combination of five bulbs while staying in budget. What should he buy? Explain why.

   _____

   _____

   _____

4. Do you think it's better to buy as many incandescent bulbs as possible or as many LED bulbs as possible. Why?

   _____

   _____

   _____

51410—180 Days of Science

Name: _____ **Date:** _____

Directions: Study the chart. Graph the lumens per watt, and answer the question.

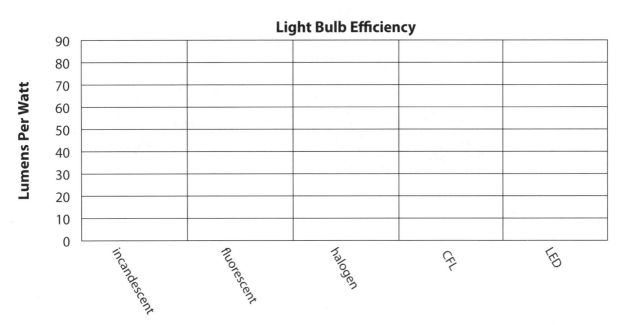

	Incandescent	Fluorescent	Halogen	CFL	LED
Lumens	850	2,600	1,200	800	800
Watts	60	40	50	13	9.5
Lumens per Watt	14	65	24	62	84

Light Bulb Efficiency

Bulb Type

1. If you can't afford LED lights, what would be your next two choices of bulbs? Why?

_____

_____

_____

Communicating Results

Name: _____ **Date:** _____

Directions: Read the text, and answer the questions.

Learning Content

Watching the Waves

If you have ever been to the beach, you have probably seen waves crashing on the shore. Waves actually move the water up and down, not forward and back. You can see this if you look at a buoy bobbing in the water. It goes up and down, but it stays in place. This pattern of up and down motion can be measured. You can measure the height of the waves and the distance between waves. The greater the height of the waves, the more energy they have.

Waves don't only happen in water. Sound and light both travel in waves. Waves transfer energy. Think about still water. You can easily walk or swim through it. However, large waves have so much energy that they can knock you over or overturn a boat.

1. What do waves transfer?

   a. energy

   b. water

   c. boats

   d. beaches

2. What travels in waves?

   a. sound

   b. water

   c. light

   d. all of the above

3. In what direction do waves move?

   a. forward and back

   b. up and down

   c. up and forward

   d. down and back

Name: _____ **Date:** _____

Directions: Read the text, and study the diagram. Then, answer the questions.

> Waves travel in patterns. The top of a wave is the crest, and the bottom of a wave is the trough. The amplitude of a wave is the distance from the middle to the crest. The wavelength is the distance between a point on one wave and the same point on the next.

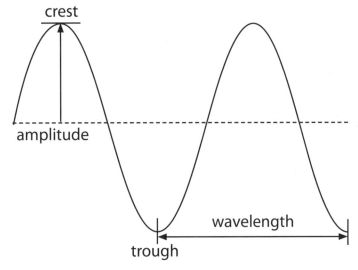

1. The amplitude is the distance from the _____ of the wave to the crest.

   a. trough

   b. middle

   c. crest

   d. wavelength

2. The distance between one trough to the next is the _____.

   a. wavelength

   b. amplitude

   c. trough

   d. crest

3. To measure wavelength, could you measure from the middle of one wave to the crest of the next? Why or why not?

   _____

   _____

4. Can the amplitude be measured from one trough to the next? Why or why not?

   _____

   _____

Analyzing Data

Name: _____   **Date:** _____

Developing Questions

Directions: Read the text, and answer the questions.

> Teresa wants to build a wave model to show the different parts of the wave. She needs something that she can bend into the right shape and that will hold its shape. She has string, wire, paper, and craft sticks.

1. Which material would be best for her wave model?

   a. string

   b. popsicle sticks

   c. wire

   d. paper

2. Which would not be part of her wave model?

   a. amplitude

   b. wavelength

   c. crest

   d. sound

3. What question could Teresa ask about building her model?

   _____

   _____

   _____

Name: _____ **Date:** _____

Directions: Read the text. Answer the questions.

Teresa wants to build a wave model to show the different parts of the wave. She is using wire because she can bend it into the right shape.

Planning Solutions

1. How can she show a greater amplitude?

    a. Make the distance from the middle of the wave to the crest larger.

    b. Make the distance from the middle of the wave to the crest smaller.

    c. Make the distance between two crests larger.

    d. Make the distance between two crests smaller.

2. How can she show a longer wavelength?

    a. Make the distance between two crests smaller.

    b. Make the distance between two crests larger

    c. Make the distance from the middle of the wave to the crest smaller.

    d. Make the distance from the middle of the wave to the crest larger.

3. What are some other ways that Teresa could explore waves?

    _____

    _____

    _____

4. What are some other materials that Teresa could use to build a wave model?

    _____

    _____

    _____

Name: _____ **Date:** _____

Directions: Draw a diagram of a wave. Label the crest, trough, amplitude, and wavelength. Then, answer the question.

Communicating Results

ABC

1. What are some things that travel in waves?

   _____

   _____

   _____

2. Is it possible for waves to move things? Why or why not?

   _____

   _____

   _____

Name: _____ **Date:** _____

Directions: Read the text, and answer the questions.

Learning Content

Morse Code

Morse Code and the telegraph were created by Samuel Morse and other inventors. Morse Code uses dots and dashes to stand for letters and numbers. The dots and dashes can be written. They can also be made with sound or light. You could beat a drum in Morse Code to send a message with sound. You could also use a flashlight to send a Morse Code message with light.

Telegraphs use Morse Code to send messages far away with electricity. The code sounds like a series of long and short clicking noises. For more than 100 years, telegraphs were the most common way to send information. They were fast and could send messages over long distances.

1. What do telegraphs use to send messages?

   a. electricity

   b. Internet

   c. light

   d. heat

2. What stands for letters in Morse code?

   a. dots

   b. dashes

   c. dots and dashes

   d. triangles

3. Do you need a telegraph to use Morse Code? Why or why not?

   _____

   _____

   _____

Name: _____ **Date:** _____

Analyzing Data

Directions: Read the text, and study the picture of Morse Code. Then, answer the questions.

Morse Code uses patterns to send messages. The dot is one second long. A dash is three seconds long. Pauses between letters are three seconds long. Pauses between words are seven seconds long.

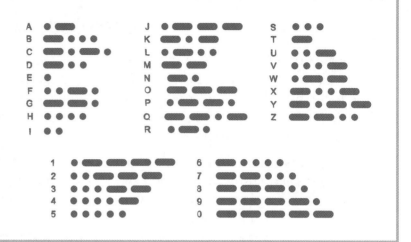

1. How many dashes are in the word "Hello"?

    a. 2   **b.** 4

    c. 5   **d.** 3

2. How many seconds long is a pause between words?

    a. 7   **b.** 3

    c. 1   **d.** 10

3. Describe the pattern you see with the numbers 1 through 9 in Morse Code.

_____

_____

_____

_____

4. Describe any other patterns you see.

_____

_____

_____

_____

Name: _____   Date: _____

Directions: Read the text, and answer the questions.

Kendra lives next door to her best friend. Their bedroom windows face each other. They decided to learn Morse Code to send messages to each other.

1. What could Kendra use to send a message in Morse Code?

   a. pillow   **b.** shoes

   c. basket ball   **d.** flashlight

2. If they don't want anyone to hear their messages, what is the best way to send them?

   a. light   **b.** sound

   c. heat   **d.** motion

3. What question could Kendra ask about the different ways she can send a Morse Code message?

   _____

   _____

   _____

4. What are several items you have at home that you could use to send messages in Morse Code?

   _____

   _____

   _____

Name: _____ **Date:** _____

Directions: Read the text, and answer the questions.

SOS is a standard emergency signal. It is …- - -… in Morse Code. Kevin goes into the car to get something for his mom. He can't get the car door back open. His mom is inside, and he wants to get his mom's attention.

1. How can Kevin get his mom's attention?

   a. Knock on the window.

   b. Use the car horn to send an SOS.

   c. Click his seatbelt.

   d. Tap on the dashboard.

2. If it was dark, what could he use to send SOS from inside the car?

   a. headlights

   b. seat belt

   c. dashboard

   d. floor mats

3. When would be the best time to use light to send Morse code, and when would be the best time to use sound? Explain why.

   _____

   _____

   _____

   _____

Name: _____ **Date:** _____

Directions: Look at the Morse Code alphabet. Write a message in the box using Morse Code, and answer the question.

1. What things do you have in your house that you could use to send messages in Morse Code?

_____

_____

_____

Communicating Results

Learning Content

Name: _____ Date: _____

Directions: Read the text, and answer the questions.

Drumbeat Signals

Drums were one of the first ways people sent messages far away. They used patterns of sounds to send these messages. They could alert others to danger, or just call everyone to gather.

The sound of some drums can reach four to five miles. This is good when people are close by. It's not as helpful if you're trying to send messages to people much farther away.

Now we can send messages far away with computers and cell phones. Technology helps messages reach people quickly. They also don't degrade, or lose quality. They send, receive, and decode information so fast that we no longer need drumbeat signals.

1. What was one of the earliest forms of long-distance communication?

    a. computers

    b. cell phones

    c. drums

    d. tablets

2. If someone is using a drum to send a message, how far away could the recipient be?

    a. a few streets over

    b. in another city

    c. in another state

    d. in another country

3. What decodes messages quickly?

    a. drums

    b. cymbals

    c. computers

    d. telegraphs

Name: _____ Date: _____

Directions: Read the text, and study the chart. Then, answer the questions.

> When you send a message, it has to be decoded. Sometimes a person does this. Sometimes technology does it for us.

Signal	Decoder
digital music	portable music player
drumbeat	human
text message	cell phone
talking on a cell phone	cell phone
Morse Code	human

1. What signals does a portable music player decode?

   a. digital music

   b. drumbeats

   c. Morse Code

   d. talking

2. Which signal is the oldest?

   a. Morse Code

   b. drumbeat

   c. digital music

   d. text message

3. What are some other signals you can think of, and what decodes them?

   _____

   _____

   _____

Developing Questions

Name: _____ **Date:** _____

Directions: Read the text, and answer the questions.

Maya and her friend are in different cities. They are talking on their phones when Maya's battery dies. They want to keep their conversation going.

1. What is the fastest form of communication they could use instead?

   a. yelling

   b. video chat

   c. writing a letter

   d. telegraph

2. If they want sound but not pictures to be part of their communication, what could they use?

   a. online voice chat

   b. writing a letter

   c. instant messaging

   d. video chat

3. What question could Maya ask about long-distance communication?

   _____

   _____

   _____

4. What forms of long-distance communication do you regularly use?

   _____

   _____

Planning Solutions

Name: _____ **Date:** _____

Directions: Read the text, and answer the questions.

Jeff likes to make videos. He usually emails them to his friends. Many of his friends live in other places.

1. When Jeff's friends view his videos on the Internet, what are their computers doing?

   a. Stopping the message.

   b. Receiving the message.

   c. Recording the message.

   d. Sending the message.

2. When different computers receive the same video, what is the result?

   a. The video message stays the same.

   b. One of the video messages will be different.

   c. All of the video messages will be different.

   d. Some of the video messages will be in a different language.

3. Besides email, what are other ways that Jeff can send videos to his friends?

_____

_____

_____

_____

Name: _____ **Date:** _____

Directions: Draw yourself sending a message over a long distance. Then, answer the questions.

[drawing box]

1. Explain what you are doing in your picture.

_____

_____

_____

2. Would the message you send lose quality by the time it gets to the recipient?

_____

_____

_____

Name: _____ **Date:** _____

Directions: Read the text, and answer the questions.

How Light Helps Us See

Without light, we cannot see. For us to see an object, light must be reflected into our eyes. Light changes direction when it reflects off an object. Every object we can see reflects some light. Mirrors reflect all light, which is why they show a good image of what they're pointed at.

Light can also be absorbed or refracted. When light is absorbed, it is stopped. Most objects absorb some light and reflect the rest. When light is refracted, the light bends. You can see this when you put a pencil or a straw in a glass of water. Rainbows are also made when light bends through water droplets in the air.

Refraction

Learning Content

1. Why can't you see objects when there is no light?

   a. No light is reflected into our eyes.

   b. Too much light is reflected into our eyes.

   c. A little bit of light is reflected into our eyes.

   d. They absorb all of the light.

2. What must reflect into our eyes for us to see?

   a. absorption

   b. darkness

   c. light

   d. refraction

3. Explain why mirrors show a good image of what they are pointed at.

   _____

   _____

   _____

Analyzing Data

Name: _____   Date: _____

Directions: Read the text, and study the chart. Then, answer the questions.

Shiny objects like mirrors reflect almost all light. Things like water and prisms can bend light. All other objects absorb most light and reflect the rest.

	Definition	Example	Example
Reflect	Light bounces off an object. All objects reflect some light. Mirrors reflect all light.	mirror	spoon
Refract	Light bends when it hits a surface.	prism	pencil in water
Absorb	Light stops and is taken in by an object. Most objects absorb most light and reflect the rest.	shirt	orange

1. What does an orange do with light?

   a. It refracts all light.

   b. It reflects all light.

   c. It refracts some light and reflects the rest.

   d. It absorbs most light and reflects the rest.

2. When something refracts light, what happens?

   a. The light stops.

   b. The light bends.

   c. The light bounces.

   d. The light disappears.

3. For an object to reflect most light, what quality should it have?

   a. dull

   b. shiny

   c. red

   d. hard

Name: _____ Date: _____

Directions: Read the text, and answer the questions.

> Stephan is playing with a mirror. It reflects the exact image of whatever he holds in front of it.
>
>

1. What is happening to the light when it hits the mirror?

   a. It is reflecting some of the light.

   b. It absorbing all of the light.

   c. It is reflecting all of the light.

   d. It is refracting the light.

2. Will a mirror work in the dark?

   a. Yes, as long as you point it at your face.

   b. No, mirrors are see-through in the dark.

   c. Yes, mirrors let us see what is in the dark.

   d. No, mirrors reflect light, and we need light to see.

3. What could Stephan ask about the mirror?

_____

_____

_____

Planning Solutions

Name: _____ **Date:** _____

Directions: Read the text, and answer the questions.

Reflection is when light bounces off an object. Because mirrors reflect all light, you can use them to bounce light onto another object. Kelly is playing with a flashlight and a mirror.

1. If Kelly shines the flashlight on the mirror and angles it toward a wall, what will happen?

   a. The light will shine on the wall.

   b. The light will turn off.

   c. The light will only show in the mirror.

   d. The light will shine on the floor.

2. If Kelly points the flashlight at a shiny object, like a spoon, what will happen?

   a. It will reflect all the light like a mirror.

   b. It will reflect most of the light.

   c. It will only reflect a little light.

   d. It will absorb all the light.

3. How can Kelly study the way that different objects reflect light?

   _____

   _____

   _____

   _____

Name: _____ **Date:** _____

Directions: Light reflects off objects and enters your eye. Draw arrows to show this, and answer the question.

light source

object

1. Explain why we cannot see in the dark.

_____

_____

_____

Name: _____ Date: _____

Directions: Read the text, and answer the questions.

Analyzing Earthquakes

Earth's surface has large masses of rock that are always slowly moving. These are called tectonic plates. As the plates move, stress can build up along fault lines, or cracks in Earth's crust. Eventually, the stress can cause the fault to suddenly slip and release the stress. This causes the ground to shake suddenly, which is an earthquake.

Earthquakes happen all the time around the world. They're often too small for people to feel. Sometimes, earthquakes are enormous. They can cause damage to property and loss of life. Earthquakes can be measured by a tool called a seismograph. This tool measures motion of the ground.

1. What are the large masses of rock called?

   a. fault lines

   b. tectonic plates

   c. earthquakes

   d. tectonic faults

2. What causes an earthquake?

   a. when a fault stops moving

   b. when a seismograph records motion

   c. when a fault suddenly slips

   d. when there is a strong storm

3. Which tool could help a scientist study an earthquake?

   a. thermometer

   b. seismograph

   c. barometer

   d. wind sock

Name: _____ Date: _____

Directions: There are many earthquakes that happen every year. Most of the time, we can't feel them at all. Study the chart, and answer the questions.

Magnitude	Earthquake Effects	Estimated Number Each Year
2.5 or less	Usually not felt, but can be recorded by seismograph.	900,000
2.5 to 5.4	Often felt, but only causes minor damage.	30,000
5.5 to 6.0	Causes slight damage to buildings and other structures.	500
6.1 to 6.9	May cause a lot of damage in very populated areas.	100
7.0 to 7.9	Major earthquake. Serious damage.	20
8.0 or greater	Great earthquake. Can totally destroy communities near the epicenter.	One every 5 to 10 years

Analyzing Data

1. What magnitude of earthquake happens least frequently?

   a. 5.5 to 6.0   b. 8.0 or greater

   c. 2.5 or less   d. 2.5 to 5.4

2. Which earthquakes are usually not felt?

   a. 2.5 or less   b. 8.0 or greater

   c. 5.5 to 6.0   d. 6.1 to 6.9

3. Which magnitude causes slight damage to buildings?

   a. 2.5 or less   b. 8.0 or greater

   c. 5.5 to 6.0   d. 6.1 to 6.9

4. Some cities are on fault lines. Do you think they are at risk for large earthquakes? Why or why not?

   _____

   _____

Name: _____ **Date:** _____

Directions: Read the text, and answer the questions.

Cora is learning about earthquakes. She learns that they happen most often at fault lines. These are cracks in the Earth's crust where rocks move against each other. The major fault lines are on the edges of the tectonic plates that make up the Earth's crust. Cora wants to know more about fault lines.

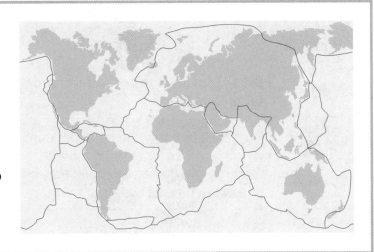

Developing Questions

1. Where do earthquakes most often happen?

   a. fault lines   **b.** underwater

   c. mountains   **d.** crust

2. Tectonic plates are the part of the Earth's _____ that move.

   a. earthquake   **b.** fault lines

   c. crust   **d.** cracks

3. Where are the major fault lines?

   _____

   _____

   _____

4. What is a question Cora could ask about tectonic plates?

   _____

   _____

   _____

Name: _____ Date: _____

Directions: Read the text, and answer the questions.

Sheila lives in Oklahoma City. One morning, she wakes up to the feeling of her bed trembling. She wonders what caused this to happen.

1. What did Sheila likely feel?

   a. tornado

   b. thunderstorm

   c. wind

   d. earthquake

2. What tool would give her more information about what she felt?

   a. something that measures movement of the earth

   b. something that measures temperature

   c. something that measures direction of wind

   d. something that measures air pressure

3. If Sheila has a doll house, how could she simulate the effects of an earthquake?

_____

_____

_____

4. Shelia's house did not have any damage after her bed trembled. Do you think what she felt was major or minor? Why or why not?

_____

_____

Communicating Results

ABC

Name: _____ **Date:** _____

Directions: Study the map, and answer the questions.

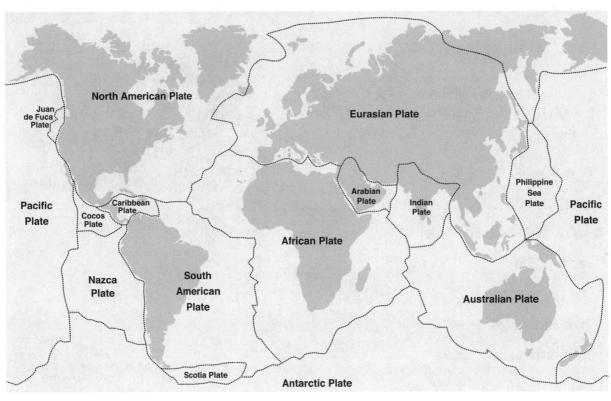

1. Why do you think that there are a lot of earthquakes in California?

_____

_____

_____

_____

2. Do you think there are a lot of earthquakes in South America? Why or why not?

_____

_____

_____

_____

_____

Name: _____ **Date:** _____

Learning Content

Directions: Read the text, and answer the questions.

Patterns in Rock Formation

The layers of rock on Earth's surface can give us a glimpse into the past. These layers are called strata. They contain information about what was happening when each layer was formed. Rock layers form from the bottom up. So, the deeper we dig, the farther back in time we can see.

Earth is about 4.6 billion years old. A lot has happened in its history. If you had a core sample of Earth, you would see layers of different colors and textures. A core sample is a section of Earth that is removed from underground with a special drill. The different layers form in different ways. This gives scientists information about what was happening at that time. Some layers were formed from extreme heat. Some were formed from magma. Some were formed by pressing sediment together over time.

1. The layers of rock on Earth are called _____ .
   a. soil
   b. strata
   c. samples
   d. textures

2. The earth is about _____ years old.
   a. 4.6 million
   b. 4,600
   c. 4.6 billion
   d. 460

3. What is a core sample?
   a. a section of Earth that shows types of weather
   b. a section of Earth removed from underground
   c. a section of Earth that is very cold
   d. a section of Earth that was pulled from the surface

4. What is different about different rock layers?

_____

_____

Name: _____ **Date:** _____

Analyzing Data

Directions: There are three types of rock. They are all formed in different ways. Study the chart, and answer the questions.

Type of Rock	What it Is
metamorphic	These rocks are formed by extreme pressure and heat. Examples include marble, slate, and quartzite.
igneous	These rocks are formed when extremely hot magma cools and solidifies. The upper section of the Earth's crust is around 95% igneous rock. Examples include granite, basalt, and obsidian.
sedimentary	These rocks are formed by sediment that is deposited over time, usually at the bottom of oceans or lakes. They form layers that are compressed over a long period of time. Examples include limestone, sandstone, and chalk.

1. Which rock is most abundant in the Earth's crust?

    a. igneous

    c. sedimentary

    b. metamorphic

    d. none of them

2. Which type of rock would be most likely to have a fossil from a fish?

    a. metamorphic

    c. igneous

    b. sedimentary

    d. none of them

3. What is something on Earth that might provide the extreme heat needed to make metamorphic rocks?

    a. a camp fire

    c. magma

    b. the sun

    d. the stars

4. Which is a type of sedimentary rock?

    a. quartzite

    c. limestone

    b. marble

    d. granite

51410—180 Days of Science

© *Shell Education*

Name: _____ **Date:** _____

Directions: Read the text, and answer the questions.

Conrad's science teacher has created some "core samples" for his class to look at. They are cups layered with different substances. Each substance stands for a layer of Earth's crust. The layers are put into the cups from oldest to newest. In one cup, there is a layer of flour on the bottom, then coffee grounds, then cornmeal, then oatmeal on top.

oatmeal

cornmeal

coffee

flour

Developing Questions

1. Which layer would be the oldest?

    a. oatmeal

    b. coffee grounds

    c. flour

    d. cornmeal

2. Which layer would be the newest?

    a. cornmeal

    b. oatmeal

    c. coffee grounds

    d. flour

3. Suppose the flour and cornmeal represent sedimentary rock, and the coffee grounds represent igneous rock. What is a question you could ask about the coffee grounds?

_____

_____

_____

_____

Planning Solutions

Name: _____   **Date:** _____

Directions: Read the text, and answer the questions.

Conrad's science teacher has created some "core samples" for his class to study. First, they study a cup with layers that stand for sedimentary rock and igneous rock. Then they look at another cup. On the bottom is cornmeal mixed with cornflakes. Coffee grounds are on top. The cornflakes represent fossils of water animals. The teacher reminds the class about the different types of rock.

igneous	cooled lava
metamorphic	changed by heat and pressure
sedimentary	sediment deposited over time, usually in oceans or lakes

1. Which type of rock does the cornmeal likely represent?

   a. sedimentary

   c. igneous

   b. metamorphic

   d. none of them

2. Suppose a volcano erupted after the fossils were deposited. Which type of rock would the coffee grounds represent?

   a. igneous

   c. metamorphic

   b. sedimentary

   d. none of them

3. Describe how you could make your own core sample model and what the different parts would be.

   _____

   _____

   _____

   _____

Name: _____ **Date:** _____

Directions: Draw a core sample. Label the oldest and newest layers. Then, answer the questions.

ABC

1. Describe the layers of your core sample.

   _____

   _____

   _____

2. Explain where the sedimentary rock usually forms.

   _____

   _____

   _____

Name: _____ **Date:** _____

Directions: Read the text, and answer the questions.

Learning from Fossils in Rock Formations

Layers of rock are a record of the past. If you dig deep enough in the right place, you will find fossils. Fossils are the preserved remains of animals or plants that lived in the past. They let us study evolution and species that have gone extinct. Fossils are the only direct way we have to learn about dinosaurs and some other animals. The parts of animals that become fossils are usually the bones or shells. The bones aren't actually bones any more. They have changed into something that is more like a stone.

1. Why do we need fossils to study certain animals?

   a. They always hide.

   b. They are extinct.

   c. They are endangered.

   d. We don't need fossils.

2. If you compared a chicken bone to a fossilized bone, would they be the same?

   a. No, the fossilized bone would be more like stone.

   b. No, the chicken bone would be more like stone.

   c. Yes, both bones would be like stone.

   d. Yes, both bones would have marrow inside.

3. Would an animal's skin usually become fossilized? Explain your answer.

   _____

   _____

   _____

Name: _____ Date: _____

Directions: There are different types of fossilization. Study the chart, and answer the questions.

Type of Fossilization	Description	Examples
perminerilzation	Substances fill the pores of shell or bone with minerals and fossilize the remains.	most dinosaur bones
resin fossilization	Organism is embedded in amber.	insect preserved in amber
carbonization	Organism is flattened between two layers of rock, and only carbon is left behind.	fossils of leaves and stems

1. What is special about resin fossilization?

   a. The whole animal is preserved.   b. Only the bones are preserved.

   c. Only the soft tissue is preserved.   d. It is the same as other fossilization.

2. Which organism could be fossilized by carbonization?

   a. dinosaur   b. fern

   c. saber tooth tiger   d. fish

3. Are dinosaur bones really bones anymore? How do you know?

   _____

   _____

Name: _____ Date: _____

Developing Questions

Directions: Read the text, and answer the questions.

Sophie is a paleontologist, which is a scientist who studies fossils. She is at a dig site looking for fossils. She finds a large bone in the ground. This is a very rare and exciting discovery. It takes a lot of time and care to remove it. She and other scientists slowly chip away at the rock around the fossil.

1. Why does it take so long to dig up a fossil?

   a. They have to be careful not to cause damage.

   b. They don't have enough people helping.

   c. They don't have the tools they need.

   d. They don't know how to properly remove the fossil.

2. Are large fossilized bones found very often?

   a. Yes, there are many of them.

   b. Yes, they are on the surface of Earth.

   c. No, they are very rare.

   d. No, people don't look for them.

3. What is a question you could ask about Sophie's discovery?

   _____

   _____

   _____

4. Why do you think Sophie works with other scientists instead of alone?

   _____

   _____

   _____

Planning Solutions

Name: _____ **Date:** _____

Directions: Read the text, and answer the questions.

Sophie is a paleontologist, which is a scientist who studies fossils. She is at a dig site with other scientists. They find a very large bone in the ground.

To find out about how old the fossil is, they are going to use relative dating. This gives the age range of a fossil instead of the exact age. This means that if they know how old the layers of rock are below and above the fossil, they can estimate its age. Some fossils called "index fossils" are helpful in relative dating. The age of these fossils is known. The animals only lived in certain time periods.

1. Relative dating will give the _____ of the fossil.

   a. exact age

   b. age range

   c. birthday

   d. date of death

2. What would be useful to have during relative dating?

   a. sediment

   b. metamorphic rock

   c. index fossils

   d. dig sites

3. If you found a fossil in a layer below an index fossil, would it be older or newer? How do you know?

_____

_____

_____

4. Would a fossil from an animal that lived a very long time be useful as an index fossil? Why or why not?

_____

_____

_____

Communicating Results

Name: _____ Date: _____

Directions: Read the text, and study the picture. Then, answer the questions.

Index fossils are helpful in relative dating. Index fossils are found in layer C. They are 300 million years old.

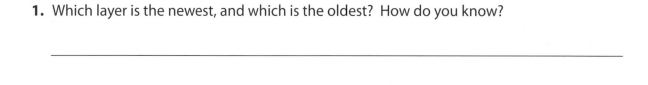

G

F

E

D

C

B

A

1. Which layer is the newest, and which is the oldest? How do you know?

   _____

   _____

   _____

2. Which layers could be used to help with relative dating? Give an example of how old those layers would be and how old the fossils around the layers could be.

   _____

   _____

   _____

Name: _____ **Date:** _____

Directions: Read the text, and answer the questions.

How Does Erosion Happen?

Erosion is when layers of Earth's surface, such as soil or rock, are worn away. When this happens, it helps mold landforms, such as seaside cliffs. The soil or rock that is worn away is deposited somewhere else. Erosion usually happens by water or wind. Water and wind can erode soil, sand, and rock. Wind can erode rocks. Erosion can also happen when water seeps into the cracks of rocks and freezes. The water expands when it freezes, and this causes the cracks to become larger. When the water freezes and thaws many times, this can break the rocks apart.

Erosion is a natural process, but humans can cause it to happen more quickly. Things like cutting down trees can make erosion worse because the roots of plants help hold soil together and prevent erosion. This can hurt the environment. It can impact beach coastlines and the quality of soil.

Learning Content

1. What is erosion?

   a. When Earth's surface is worn away.

   b. When Earth's surface is underwater.

   c. When Earth's surface is built up.

   d. When Earth's surface is covered in ice.

2. Erosion can be caused by _____ , _____ , or _____ .

   a. water, ice, environment

   b. water, soil, rocks

   c. water, wind, ice

   d. water, wind, rocks

3. What is something humans do to make erosion happen more quickly?

   _____

   _____

Analyzing Data

Name: _____   Date: _____

Directions: Erosion helps shape the land. This process happens over a long period of time. Study the pictures, and answer the questions.

1. What is likely eroding this beach?

   a. seagulls

   b. humans

   c. water

   d. none of these

2. How long might it take for this arch to form?

   a. 200 years

   b. 2 weeks

   c. 2 days

   d. 2 months

3. What might happen to the arch over time?

   _____

   _____

   _____

   _____

4. What else could contribute to the erosion of the arch?

   _____

Name: _____ Date: _____

Directions: Read the text, and answer the questions.

Zack notices that grass has died on the side of his house where it is always shady. Eventually, the grass is gone, and there is only dirt. The dirt starts to pull away from the foundation of the house.

Developing Questions

1. What is happening to the dirt around the foundation of the house?

   a. It is eroding.   **b.** It is growing.

   c. It has chemicals in it.   **d.** It is being developed.

2. What is the reason that the dirt is receding?

   a. There is no grass to hold the soil in place.   **b.** Zack dug a hole in the dirt.

   c. An animal moved the dirt.   **d.** The foundation pushed it away.

3. What is a question Zack could ask about the role of plants in preventing erosion?

   _____

   _____

   _____

4. What is something Zack could do to prevent more erosion?

   _____

   _____

   _____

Name: _____ **Date:** _____

Directions: Read the text, and answer the questions.

Planning Solutions

Dawn is a farmer. The soil on her farm is eroding between planting seasons from a lot of heavy rain. If too much soil erodes, the land will lose nutrients that are important to plants. She decides to plant cover crops, like oats, which help manage soil erosion with their roots.

1. Why does it matter if the soil loses nutrients?

   a. Plants won't have what they need to grow.

   b. Plants will have too much of what they need.

   c. The soil can't absorb water.

   d. The soil will absorb too much water.

2. How do cover crops prevent soil erosion?

   a. Their roots hold soil together.

   b. They make the soil very loose.

   c. Their leaves shade the soil.

   d. They do not stop soil erosion.

3. Would a large crop of oats or a single tree make a better cover crop? Explain your answer.

   _____

   _____

   _____

4. How can Dawn learn about additional ways to stop erosion on her farm?

   _____

   _____

   _____

Earth and Space Science

Name: _____ Date: _____

Directions: Draw a picture of a place before and after erosion. Label your pictures. Then, answer the questions.

Before Erosion

After Erosion

1. Explain the effects of erosion in your picture.

_____

_____

2. Would this erosion happen over a long or short period of time? Why?

_____

_____

Learning Content

Name: _____ **Date:** _____

Directions: Read the text, and answer the questions.

Water Erosion

Moving water is the main cause of erosion. Erosion is when Earth's surface is worn away. It can be caused by rain when it hits the surface. The water flows in small streams and carries soil away. Erosion can also be caused by rivers. They break up rocks along the riverbed and carry the material downstream. Rivers can even carve valleys and canyons over time. The Grand Canyon was created by the Colorado River over a long period of time. Ocean waves can cause the coastline to erode. The rock and sand is deposited in other places. This changes the shapes of coastlines.

1. Can a puddle of water erode soil?

   a. Yes, if it is still.

   b. No, only water erodes soil.

   c. Yes, if it is moving.

   d. No, water does not erode soil.

2. What can the moving water from rivers create?

   a. valleys

   b. canyons

   c. hills

   d. both a and b

3. What happens to pieces of rock and sand that are eroded?

   a. They are deposited somewhere else.

   b. They stay where they came from.

   c. They are carried away by birds.

   d. They are buried underground.

Name: _____ Date: _____

Directions: Read the text, and study the chart. Then, answer the questions.

Rain erosion is caused when bits of soil are moved by raindrops. Sheet erosion is when a thin layer of soil is removed from a large area. Rill and gully erosion is when streams of water cause small or large channels to form. Channel erosion causes stream beds and banks to change shape.

Types of Water Erosion

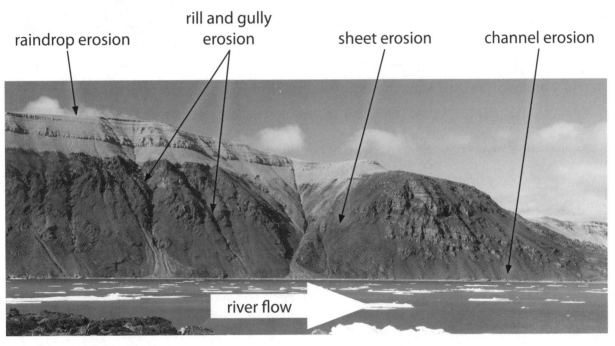

raindrop erosion rill and gully erosion sheet erosion channel erosion

river flow

1. Which type of erosion removes a thin layer of soil from a large area?

   a. raindrop

   c. rill and gully

   b. sheet

   d. channel

2. What shapes the banks of a stream or river?

   a. channel erosion

   c. raindrop erosion

   b. sheet erosion

   d. rill and gully erosion

3. What might happen to the stream over time?

   _____

   _____

   _____

Developing Questions

Name: _____ **Date:** _____

Directions: Read the text, and answer the questions.

Olivia is visiting the Grand Canyon with her family. She learns that it took six million years to form. It was carved by the Colorado River. The canyon is over one mile deep and 277 miles long.

1. The Colorado River still flows through the Grand Canyon. Is erosion still happening?

   a. Yes, because the water is still moving.

   b. No, the canyon has gotten as deep as possible.

   c. Yes, but only from wind.

   d. No, the water is not moving.

2. If the Colorado River dried up, what would happen?

   a. The erosion of the Grand Canyon would increase.

   b. The erosion of the Grand Canyon would be greatly reduced.

   c. The Grand Canyon would fill with soil.

   d. The Grand Canyon would triple in size.

3. What could Olivia ask about the process of eroding rock?

   _____

   _____

   _____

4. Do you think the Grand Canyon used to be deeper or more shallow? Why?

   _____

   _____

   _____

51410—180 Days of Science

Name: _____ **Date:** _____

Directions: Read the text, and answer the questions.

Alexander lives in Louisiana. He is studying beach erosion. It is caused by waves and currents. The sand that is washed away is deposited into sandbars, which are ridges of sand that build up in the water. He learns that the Louisiana coastline is eroding at a rate of 16 square miles per year.

Planning Solutions

1. Do all ocean coastlines erode?

   a. Yes, because there are waves and currents at every beach.

   b. No, there are only waves and currents in Louisiana.

   c. Yes, but wind is the only cause of erosion at other beaches.

   d. No, some beaches have sand that won't move.

2. If you swim to deeper water at the beach and find a place that is suddenly more shallow, what did you find?

   a. a wave

   b. a current

   c. a coastline

   d. a sandbar

3. Make a plan for Alexander to learn if the rate of beach erosion in Louisiana is normal.

   _____

   _____

   _____

   _____

Communicating Results

Name: _____ Date: _____

Directions: Label the diagram using words from the word bank. Then, answer the question.

| raindrop erosion | sheet erosion | rill and gully erosion | channel erosion |

Types of Water Induced Erosion

_____ Small bits of soil are moved.

_____ Streams cause channels to form.

A thin layer of soil is removed from a large area.

This causes stream beds to change shape.

river flow

1. What could happen if the sheet erosion continues?

_____

_____

_____

_____

2. What could happen if the rill and gully erosion continues?

_____

_____

_____

_____

Name: _____   Date: _____

Directions: Read the text, and answer the questions.

Wind Erosion

Wind erosion is when wind causes Earth's surface to wear away. Wind can carry dust, sand, soil, and volcanic ash to far-away places. Wind can blow away layers of top soil on farms. This hurts plants and the quality of the soil. A lot of wind erosion happens in desert climates. In these areas, there are not many plants to hold the soil together. This makes it easier for wind to blow sand away.

When sand and dust blow against rocks, it can slowly wear them away. This can create beautiful rock formations with smooth sides. Arches National Park in Utah is one place where wind erosion shaped the rock. Over millions of years, even mountains can be worn away until almost nothing remains.

1. Where is wind erosion common?

a. forests

b. grasslands

c. deserts

d. oceans

2. What blows against rocks to wear them away?

a. sand and dust

b. water and ice

c. ice and snow

d. grass and leaves

3. Will mountains change shape over time? Why or why not?

_____

_____

4. Why can wind erosion be a problem?

_____

_____

Analyzing Data

Name: _____ **Date:** _____

Directions: Read the text, and study the chart. Then, answer the questions.

> When there are fewer plants, there is more wind erosion. To control erosion, at least half of the ground must be covered with trees or grass.

Amount of Ground Covered by Plants	Amount of Soil Eroded
all	none
4/5	1/30
3/5	1/20
2/5	1/10
1/5	1/4
none	4/5

1. How much of the ground needs to be covered to control erosion?

   a. 3/4   **b.** 1/2

   c. 1/4   **d.** 1/10

2. How much soil will be eroded by wind if the ground is completely covered with plants?

   a. none   **b.** half

   c. most   **d.** all

3. If there is no ground cover at all, how will wind affect the soil?

   _____

   _____

4. How does erosion change as ground cover increases?

   _____

   _____

   _____

Name: _____ **Date:** _____

Developing Questions

Directions: Read the text, and answer the questions.

> Noah visits the Arches National Park in Utah. The park has more than 2,000 amazing arches. They are made of red sandstone rocks. They look like they were carved by people. Noah was surprised to learn that wind erosion, not people, created the arches. The arches took millions of years to form.

1. What created the arches?

    a. wind erosion   **b.** people

    c. animals   **d.** sunlight

2. How long did the arches take to form?

    a. 2 years   **b.** 200 years

    c. millions of years   **d.** thousands of years

3. What could Noah ask about the process of wind erosion?

_____

_____

_____

Planning Solutions

Name: _____ Date: _____

Directions: Read the text, and answer the questions.

> Chris wants to set up a wind erosion experiment. He has dirt, a plastic container, straws, and a hairdryer. He puts dirt in a container to represent Earth's surface.

1. Chris uses one straw to blow air gently on the dirt. This could represent a _____ .

   a. light breeze

   b. strong gust

   c. wind storm

   d. strong wind

2. How could Chris simulate a stronger wind?

   a. Blow harder with two straws.

   b. Stick a straw in the dirt.

   c. Put ice cubes on the dirt.

   d. Pour water on the dirt.

3. What could Chris to do simulate the effects of a strong wind storm?

   _____

   _____

   _____

4. If you added something to the dirt, like plants or buildings, do you think it would change the results? Why or why not?

   _____

   _____

Name: _____   Date: _____

Directions: Draw your own rock formation created by wind erosion. Answer the question.

1. Describe how your rock formation was created.

_____

_____

_____

Name: _____ **Date:** _____

Directions: Read the text, and answer the questions.

Using Topographic Maps

Topographic maps show us the shape of Earth's surface. They look a lot different from a regular map. Regular maps show mostly highways and roads. Topographic maps show a more realistic view of the landscape. They let you see the 3D landscape on a 2D surface. This means that they show things like the height of mountains and the depth of valleys. They may also show lakes and streams. They have a lot of different lines and symbols, which means that they are different to read than a regular map. The curved lines are called contour lines. These are what show the height of the land. Because these maps have so much information, you can use them for many different things. They are very useful for hiking and other outdoor activities.

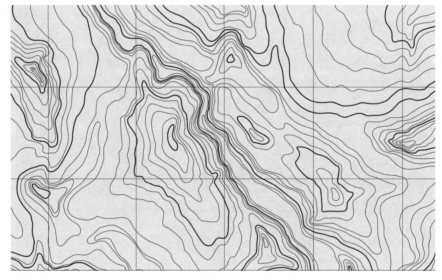

1. What do contour lines tell you?

    a. the location of trees

    b. the location of rivers

    c. the height of the land

    d. the location of roads

2. What can a topographic map show?

    a. depth of valleys

    b. plants on a mountain

    c. animals on a mountain

    d. ice on a mountain

3. For which activity would a topographic map be useful?

    a. driving

    b. swimming

    c. hiking

    d. basketball

Learning Content

Name: _____ Date: _____

Directions: Read the text, and study the map. Then, answer the questions.

> Topographic maps have curved lines called contour lines. They tell you the elevation of the land. Elevation is the height above sea level. Every point of a contour line has the same elevation. They close to form circles. The tops of mountains or hills are marked with crosses. When contour lines are close together, that means the land is steep. When the lines are far apart the land is more flat.

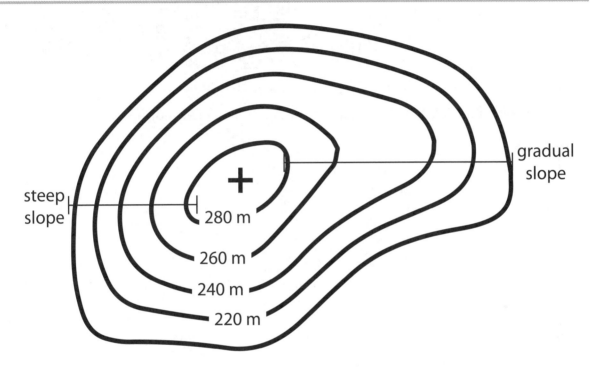

1. What are the curved lines called?

   a. topographic lines

   c. map lines

   b. contour lines

   d. elevation lines

2. What do the lines on the map represent?

   a. elevation

   c. rivers

   b. trees

   d. roads

3. How can you tell if a hill is steep?

   _____

   _____

   _____

Developing Questions

Name: _____ Date: _____

Directions: Read the text, and answer the questions.

Jenny is hiking with her family. They want to stay at the same elevation the whole time. They are using a topographic map to help them.

1. What should they follow on the map to stay at the same elevation?

   a. roads

   b. hills

   c. contour lines

   d. rivers

2. The map has 280 m written on a small contour line with a cross inside it. What does it mean?

   a. It is a hill 280 m high.

   b. It is a valley 280 m deep.

   c. It is a river 280 m long.

   d. It is a canyon 280 m wide.

3. What could Jenny ask about reading a topographic map?

   _____

   _____

   _____

4. What is another way the topographic map could be used for their hike?

   _____

   _____

Planning Solutions

Name: _____ **Date:** _____

Directions: Read the text, and answer the questions.

Jenny is hiking with her family. She sees mountains on their topographic map. There are many contour lines close together around the mountains. She also sees a river. There are no contour lines near the river.

1. There are no contour lines around the river because the ground is _____ .

    a. flat   **b.** steep

    c. deep   **d.** low

2. If the contour lines are close together, it means the ground is _____ .

    a. soft   **b.** steep

    c. flat   **d.** rocky

3. How can Jenny use the topographic map to plan their hike?

    _____

    _____

    _____

4. Can the map tell Jenny how difficult a hill would be to climb? Explain your answer.

    _____

    _____

    _____

Name: _____ **Date:** _____

Communicating Results

Directions: Add features to the topographic map using symbols from the map legend. Then, answer the questions.

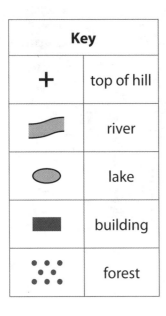

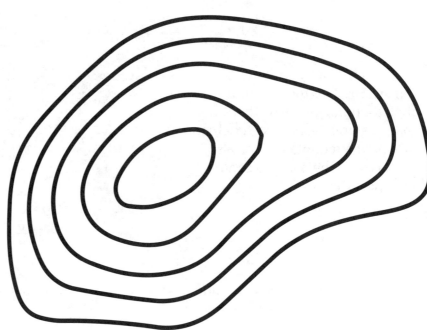

Key	
+	top of hill
～	river
⬭	lake
▬	building
∵∴	forest

1. How would you use a topographic map?

_____

_____

_____

2. Describe the area that your map shows.

_____

_____

_____

3. When would someone use your map?

_____

_____

_____

Name: _____ **Date:** _____

Directions: Read the text, and answer the questions.

Volcanoes and Earthquake

Most of the world's volcanoes happen along the boundaries of Earth's tectonic plates. These are the large slabs of slowly moving rock that make up Earth's crust. Volcanoes happen here because the space between the plates allows magma to flow to the surface. This is also where most earthquakes happen. If you plot all of Earth's volcanoes and earthquakes on a map, you will see this pattern.

There are several big fault lines that form something called the Pacific Ring of Fire. It runs around the Pacific Ocean. Here you can find many volcanoes and earthquakes. There are also ocean trenches and mountain trenches. These are all created by Earth's moving plates.

1. Where do most earthquakes and volcanoes occur?

a. in deserts

b. between tectonic plates

c. in Japan

d. in the Atlantic Ocean

2. You can find earthquakes, volcanoes, ocean trenches, and mountain trenches along the _____ .

a. volcano belt

b. earthquake band

c. Atlantic Ring of Fire

d. Pacific Ring of Fire

3. Explain what a tectonic plate is.

_____

_____

_____

4. What is the Pacific Ring of Fire?

_____

_____

Analyzing Data

Name: _____ **Date:** _____

Directions: Read the text, and study the map. Then, answer the questions.

> The Pacific Ring of Fire is made up of plate boundaries. It wraps around the Pacific Ocean. There are many volcanoes and ocean trenches at the plate boundaries. Many earthquakes happen here. The Pacific Ring of fire is 25,000 miles long.

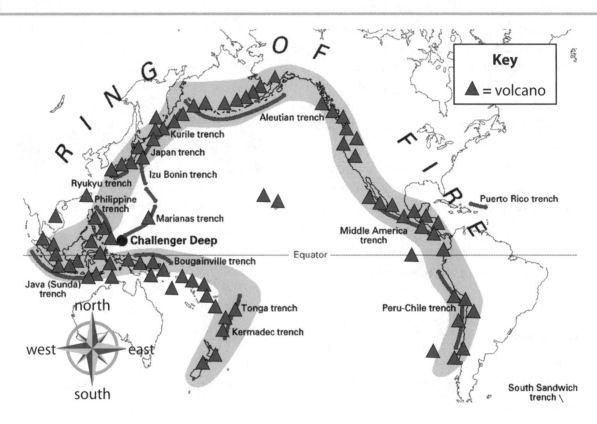

1. The _____ and _____ are near the Pacific Ring of Fire.

   a. rivers and volcanoes

   c. mountains and ponds

   b. Aleutian Trench and Japan Trench

   d. Chinese Trench and South American Trench

2. What land formations are around the Pacific Ring of Fire besides volcanoes?

   a. trenches

   c. cliffs

   b. deserts

   d. waterfalls

3. What do the triangles on the map represent?

   _____

Name: _____ Date: _____

Directions: Read the text, and answer the questions.

Jose is looking at a map of volcanoes in the United States. He finds out that there are 169 active volcanoes there. They are marked with different color triangles on the map. Most of them are in Alaska. They erupt almost every year. Jose wants to learn more about the volcanoes.

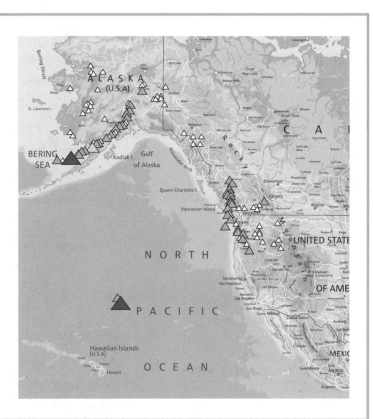

1. What feature of Earth would have the most volcanoes near it?

   a. plate boundaries   **b.** valleys

   c. hills   **d.** desert

2. What color and size of triangle would you use to label a volcano that might erupt soon? Why?

   _____

   _____

   _____

3. What is a question Jose could ask about the volcanoes in Alaska?

   _____

   _____

   _____

Planning Solutions

Name: _____   **Date:** _____

Directions: Read the text, and answer the questions.

Jose is looking at a map of volcanoes in the United States. He finds out that there are 169 active volcanoes in the country. There are 93 of them in Alaska. Volcanoes in Alaska erupt almost every year. Jose wants to understand why.

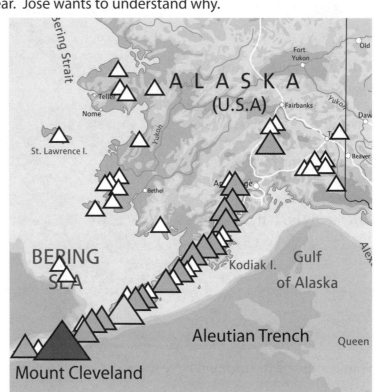

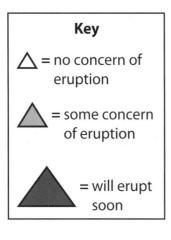

Key

△ = no concern of eruption

◭ = some concern of eruption

▲ = will erupt soon

1. Near which geographic feature are most of Alaska's volcanoes?

   a. Brooks Range
   b. Aleutian Trench

   c. California
   d. Canada

2. What is important to know about Mount Cleveland?

   a. It will erupt soon.
   b. It will never erupt.

   c. It might erupt soon.
   d. It very recently erupted.

3. Make a plan for Jose to learn more about Mount Cleveland.

_____

_____

_____

Name: _____ **Date:** _____

Directions: Graph the number of volcanoes in each state. Then, answer the question.

State	Number of Volcanoes
Alaska	93
Arizona	3
California	20
Colorado	1
Hawaii	5
Idaho	4

State	Number of Volcanoes
Oregon	19
Nevada	4
New Mexico	4
Utah	5
Washington	10
Wyoming	1

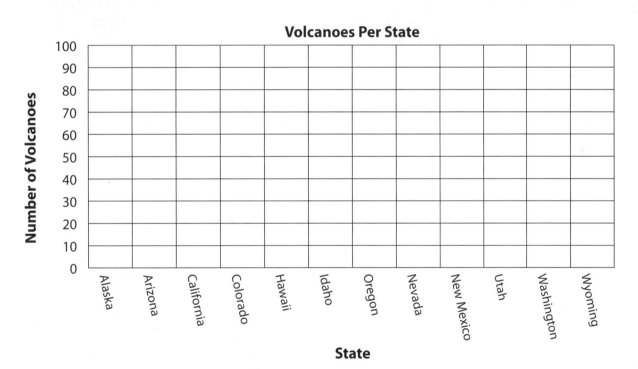

Volcanoes Per State

1. Besides Alaska, which three states have the most volcanoes?

_____

_____

_____

Communicating Results

Name: _____ **Date:** _____

Directions: Read the text, and answer the questions.

The Costs and Benefits of Dams

Dams are built across streams and rivers to block the flow of water. They have many uses. They can provide lakes for swimming, boating, and fishing. They can collect water for us to drink, for watering land, or for use in factories. They can keep rivers from flooding or create deeper water for ships to travel. They can also be a source of energy called hydroelectric power. Many dams are used for several things at once. Although there can be many benefits to dams, there can be downsides as well.

Sometimes dams can hurt animals by taking away their homes. Some animals, like salmon, can't migrate to reproduce when a dam is built across a river. Dams can make land less fertile. They can even cause flooding in certain areas.

1. What is the basic function of a dam?

    a. To drain water.   **b.** To flood an area.

    c. To increase the flow of water.   **d.** To block the flow of water.

2. Dams can be a source of energy called _____ power.

    a. hydroelectric   **b.** industrial

    c. irrigation   **d.** river

3. Dams can collect water for what purpose?

    a. watering land   **b.** drinking

    c. swimming   **d.** all of the above

4. How can dams hurt the environment?

_____

_____

_____

Learning Content

Name: _____ Date: _____

Directions: This diagram shows how the energy from moving water can be turned into electricity. Study the diagram, and answer the questions.

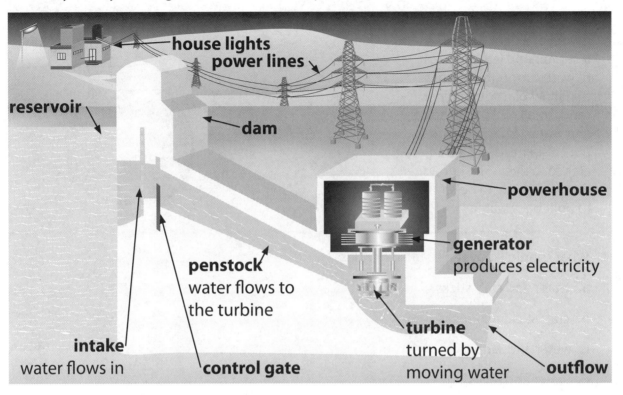

1. Where does the water flow into the dam?

   a. outflow   **b.** generator

   c. intake   **d.** powerhouse

2. What does the water turn to create electricity?

   a. turbine   **b.** power lines

   c. outflow   **d.** powerhouse

3. What is the pipeline called that leads to the turbine?

   a. control cate   **b.** reservoir

   c. penstock   **d.** outflow

4. After electricity is created, where does it go?

   _____

   _____

Developing Questions

Name: _____ Date: _____

Directions: Read the text, and answer the questions.

Libby wants to make a model of a dam that has a reservoir and lets a little bit of water through. She has a shallow plastic container, sand, small rocks, craft sticks, and water. She puts sand in the container and digs an area for a river. She knows the dam needs to be strong to hold back water.

1. What should Libby use to build her dam?

   a. water and craft sticks

   b. craft sticks and rocks

   c. water and sand

   d. water and rocks

2. If the dam blocks all instead of some of the water, what could Libby do?

   a. Leave large openings in her dam.

   b. Leave very small openings in her dam.

   c. Build stairs over her dam.

   d. Add a sidewalk next to her dam.

3. What could Jenny ask about improving the dam?

   _____

   _____

   _____

   _____

51410—180 Days of Science

Name: _____ Date: _____

Directions: Read the text, and answer the questions.

Leroy is learning that dams can sometimes have negative effects on the environment. Fish like salmon migrate so that they can spawn, or lay eggs. Salmon have to spawn in certain areas. Dams can block them from swimming where they need to go. Dams can also kill animals by changing their habitat.

Planning Solutions

1. Why is it bad that salmon are blocked from migrating?

    a. They can't get to their spawning habitat.

    b. They can't visit their family.

    c. They can't find food.

    d. It isn't bad. They can spawn anywhere.

2. If a dam changes the temperature of a river, what could happen?

    a. The river will change color.

    b. The river will smell different.

    c. Some plants and animals may die.

    d. Nothing will change.

3. Make a plan for Leroy to find out how some dams are designed to let salmon pass through.

_____

_____

_____

4. If an animal dies out because of a dam, do you think it could affect other plants and animals? Why or why not?

_____

_____

_____

Name: _____   Date: _____

Communicating Results

Directions: Some effects of building dams are listed in the box. Decide if each effect is positive or negative, and write it in the chart.

provides water for irrigation
changes animal habitats
makes hydroelectric power
creates lakes for recreation
supplies drinking water
can cause flooding in flat areas
can make land less fertile downstream
can prevent flooding

Positive ✓	Negative ✕

Name: _____ Date: _____

Directions: Read the text, and answer the questions.

Wind Power

The wind is a strong force of nature. We can harness the power of wind and use it to make electricity. The kinetic energy of wind can be converted into electrical energy. This happens when wind blows turbines. The turbines drive a generator that creates electricity. The electricity is then sent to power lines that carry electricity to buildings.

Wind power is a renewable source of energy, which means it never runs out. The power of wind has been used for hundreds of years. Windmills were used for grinding grains and pumping water. Now there are large wind farms that generate a large amount of power. The best places for wind farms are in areas where there is a lot of wind. The use of wind power has increased in recent years.

1. Wind blows _____ to convert kinetic energy into electricity.

   a. water

   b. renewable

   c. kinetic

   d. turbines

2. What kind of energy is wind power?

   a. renewable

   b. non-renewable

   c. fossil fuel

   d. hydroelectric

3. Are places without a lot of wind good for wind farms?

   a. Yes, the air needs to be still.

   b. No, windy places are best.

   c. Yes, as long as there is lots of sun.

   d. No, cloudy places are the best.

4. What happens to electricity once it is created on a wind farm?

_____

_____

_____

Learning Content

Analyzing Data

Name: _____ Date: _____

Directions: Read the text, and study the diagram. Then, answer the questions.

> Wind turbines take up a lot of space. They are hundreds of feet tall. The cost of this type of energy is similar to coal and gas, but wind power does not pollute the air.

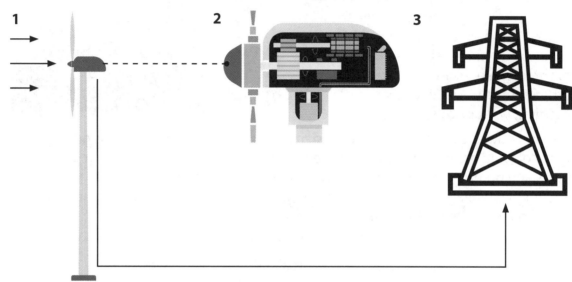

How Wind Energy Works

(1) Wind turns blades of the wind turbine.

(2) Turbines turn generators, making electricity.

(3) Electricity is sent to buildings to be used.

1. What part of the wind turbine does the wind move?

   a. blades

   b. turbine

   c. generator

   d. buildings

2. What converts wind to electricity?

   a. blades

   b. generator

   c. buildings

   d. turbine

3. Where does the electricity go after it is created?

   a. blades

   b. air

   c. water

   d. buildings

Name: _____ Date: _____

Directions: Read the text, and answer the questions.

Niko has a pinwheel. It is a windy day. He takes the pinwheel outside, and every time the wind gusts, the pinwheel spins very fast. When the wind slows down, so does the pinwheel.

1. Kinetic energy from the wind is _____ the pinwheel.

    a. stopping   **b.** transferring to

    c. pulling on   **d.** giving electricity to

2. What is the pinwheel like?

    a. wind turbine   **b.** substation

    c. power grid   **d.** kite

3. What could Niko ask about the connections between the pinwheel and wind turbines?

_____

_____

_____

4. What are some other toys or activities that would need wind to work?

_____

_____

_____

Name: _____ **Date:** _____

Planning Solutions

Directions: Read the text, and answer the questions.

> Myra wants to build a wind-powered car. She wants to build a car that has a sail. The wind can blow the sail and move the car. She has straws, hard candy rings, paper, and tape.

1. What should she use for the sail?

   a. paper

   c. candy rings

   b. tape

   d. straws

2. When wind blows the car, _____ energy is being transferred to the car.

   a. chemical

   c. kinetic

   b. heat

   d. electric

3. How should Myra build her car?

   _____

   _____

   _____

4. Do you think the size of the sail would affect how the car works? Why or why not?

   _____

   _____

   _____

Name: _____ Date: _____

Directions: Wind turbines are used to create electricity. Fill out the flow chart with the steps in the correct order. Then, answer the question.

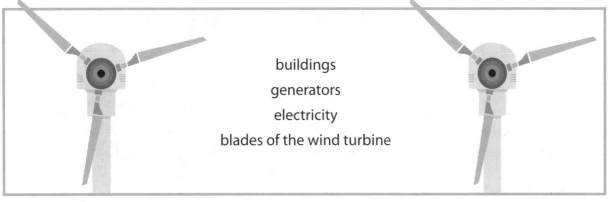

buildings

generators

electricity

blades of the wind turbine

Step 1

Wind turns _____ .

↓

Step 2

Turbines turn _____ , which makes _____ .

↓

Step 3

Electricity is sent to _____ to be used.

1. What are three things that the wind electricity could be used for?

_____

_____

_____

2. Is wind energy a renewable source of energy? Why or why not?

_____

_____

_____

Communicating Results

ABC

Name: _____ Date: _____

Learning Content

Directions: Read the text, and answer the questions.

Reducing the Impact of Tsunamis

Tsunamis are huge waves that often occur after earthquakes or volcanic eruptions in the ocean. They are also called seismic sea waves. Although they are a natural occurrence, they can be devastating to humans. They can destroy entire towns and the land where they hit. The waves start in deep water. They move very fast. They can travel as fast as 800 kilometers (500 miles) per hour. The waves become much higher as they approach the shore. They can be as high as 30 meters (about 100 feet) before they crash to the shore.

We can't stop tsunamis from happening, but we can help limit their damage. Awareness programs and early warning systems help save lives. Flood areas are also known, which helps keep people out of harm's way.

1. Do people always have a lot of warning before a tsunami?

   a. Yes, because they travel slowly.

   b. No, because no one knows how they happen.

   c. Yes, everyone receives warnings instantly.

   d. No, because they move very fast.

2. Why can tsunamis be devastating?

   a. The waves are huge.

   b. They travel fast.

   c. They cause flooding.

   d. all of the above

3. What are some ways that people can limit the damage caused by tsunamis?

   _____

   _____

4. Why is it important to know that tsunami waves travel so fast?

   _____

   _____

Name: _____ Date: _____

Directions: This chart shows ways people can limit tsunami damage. Study the chart, and answer the questions.

Technique	Result
detection and early warning system	People know that a tsunami will happen. They have time to evacuate. They can predict when the tsunami will hit and how large it will be.
tsunami hazard maps	Maps show areas prone to flooding. Maps are consulted when building to help keep people and critical buildings out of flood zones.
tsunami awareness programs	Community is educated about tsunami dangers.
creation of evacuation procedures	There are marked routes for people to evacuate.

Analyzing Data

1. Which technique helps people understand the dangers of tsunamis?

   a. hazard maps

   b. evacuation procedures

   c. awareness programs

   d. early warning systems

2. What helps people decide where to build houses?

   a. hazard maps

   b. evacuation procedures

   c. early warning systems

   d. awareness programs

3. What are some types of early warnings that could be used to alert people about a tsunami?

   _____

   _____

   _____

Developing Questions

Name: _____   Date: _____

Directions: Read the text, and answer the questions.

Rosa is thinking of ways to reduce damage from tsunamis. She knows that they can sometimes be spotted early. She reads about special buoys that sense earthquakes at the bottom of the sea. They send this information to areas that could be affected. She is trying to figure out a good warning system for these areas.

1. Which would be the most effective way to warn people?

   a. word of mouth

   b. billboards

   c. outdoor sirens

   d. postcards

2. What are some additional warning methods that you think would help warn the most people?

   _____

   _____

   _____

   _____

3. What could Rosa ask about tsunami warning systems?

   _____

   _____

   _____

   _____

Name: _____ Date: _____

Directions: Read the text, and answer the questions.

Rex is reading about tsunami awareness programs. They are made to help people know what to do in case of a tsunami. There are official warnings, like sirens. There are also natural warnings, like long or strong earthquakes. People should know how to recognize both.

1. If you are near the beach and feel an earthquake, what should you do?

   a. Get away from the water.

   b. Go into the ocean.

   c. Watch the waves.

   d. Wait for instructions.

2. Which types of materials could be used to educate the public about tsunamis?

   a. TV commercials

   b. signs

   c. school programs

   d. all of these

3. What do you think would be a good way to educate the public about tsunami warning signs?

   _____

   _____

   _____

   _____

Name: _____ Date: _____

Directions: Create your own tsunami hazard map. Show the areas that are likely to flood if there was a tsunami. Label your map. Then, answer the question.

Communicating Results

1. Explain the most important parts of your map.

_____

_____

_____

Learning Content

Name: _____ **Date:** _____

Directions: Read the text, and answer the questions.

Predicting Volcanic Eruptions and Earthquakes

Volcanoes and earthquakes are unpredictable. At any moment, the ground could shake. Lava could explode into the sky. Scientists can make predictions about when these things will happen. They aren't always that accurate, though. Its easiest for scientists to predict the location of these events. Scientists know where most earthquakes will happen based on the location of fault lines. Many known volcanoes are monitored every day. Knowing the exact time that earthquakes and eruptions will happen is a lot harder.

Knowing the history of volcanoes and fault lines is a big help. Sometimes scientists know an event will happen soon because they happen on a fairly regular schedule. Things like the movement and shape of the ground can give clues, too. None of these things give us all the answers. Nature always has the final say.

1. What is easiest for scientists to predict?

   a. the time of an earthquake

   b. the day of an earthquake

   c. the location of an earthquake

   d. the strength of an earthquake

2. To predict a volcanic eruption, scientists should use _____.

   a. schedules

   b. a variety of methods

   c. textbooks

   d. all of the above

3. What are the benefits of being able to predict volcanic eruptions or earthquakes?

_____

_____

_____

Analyzing Data

Name: _____ Date: _____

Directions: Read the text, and study the chart. Then, answer the questions.

Scientists track several things to help know when a volcano will erupt. The more things they track, the better. When they have more information, they can make more accurate predictions.

Event Tracked	What it Means
history of eruption	If a volcano erupts on a fairly regular schedule, scientists know when an eruption is more likely to happen.
movement of the ground	A change or increase in ground movement can mean a volcano will erupt soon.
ground deformation	Before an eruption, the ground near a volcano can begin to swell as magma rises up.
vapors	A change or increase in gasses coming out of a volcano could mean an eruption is coming.

1. What could a large, sudden increase in ground movement mean?

   a. The volcano will erupt soon.

   b. The volcano will erupt in 10 years.

   c. The volcano is not active.

   d. The volcano erupted last week.

2. What does ground deformation mean?

   a. Gasses are coming from the volcano.

   b. The ground is changing shape.

   c. Earthquakes are happening.

   d. The volcano hasn't erupted in 10 years.

3. A volcano has a history of erupting every 50 years. It has been 60 years since the last eruption. What does this mean?

   _____

   _____

Name: _____ **Date:** _____

Directions: Read the text, and answer the questions.

> Jamir is learning about earthquakes. He finds out that they are very hard to predict. Scientists do have tools that can help. Seismometers can pick up vibrations from Earth that might increase before an earthquake. Jamir wants to learn more about seismometers.

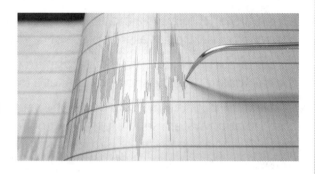

1. A seismometer is a tool that picks up _____ from Earth.

    a. vibrations

    b. radon gas

    c. plates

    d. cracks

2. Could Jamir predict an earthquake?

    a. Yes, anyone can predict an earthquake.

    b. Yes, because he learned about earthquakes at school.

    c. No, they are even hard for scientists to predict.

    d. No, he needs to go to high school first.

3. What can Jamir ask about seismometers?

    _____

    _____

    _____

4. What kind of line do you think a seismometer would create if it detects a strong vibration? Why?

    _____

    _____

    _____

Name: _____ Date: _____

Planning Solutions

Directions: Read the text, and answer the questions.

Jamir wants to build a model of an earthquake-resistant building. He uses a shoe box for a house. He has a large piece of cardboard for the ground.

Jamir puts the large piece of cardboard on a table with the box on top. He shakes the cardboard, and the shoe box shakes a lot.

Next, he puts the markers under the shoe box to act as a base isolation system. A base isolation system separates a building from the ground to keep it from shaking as much during an earthquake. Jamir shakes the cardboard again. The shoe box shakes less.

Base Isolation System

1. When the shoe box is on the cardboard "ground," why does it move a lot?

   a. It is directly on the moving ground.

   b. It is isolated from the moving ground.

   c. It is floating above the moving ground.

   d. It is inside the moving ground.

2. How does the base isolation system help the shoe box "house" move less?

   a. It isolates the base of the house from the movement of the ground.

   b. It makes the building stronger.

   c. It tells people to leave the building during an earthquake.

   d. It prevents the building from moving at all.

3. How could Jamir improve his design by adding other shock-absorbing materials (like cotton balls, rubber bands, string, and springs)?

   _____

   _____

   _____

Name: _____ Date: _____

Directions: Study the pictures. Circle the base isolation system, and answer the questions.

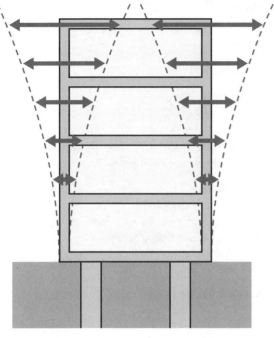

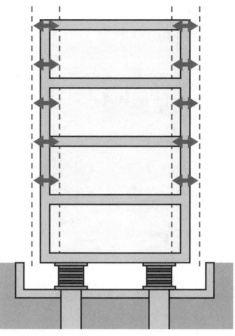

Without Base Isolation System   **With Base Isolation System**

1. What is the main difference between the two buildings during an earthquake?

_____

_____

_____

2. How does the base isolation system affect the building during an earthquake?

_____

_____

_____

3. What are some benefits of base isolation systems in areas that have earthquakes?

_____

_____

_____

Communicating Results

ABC

Answer Key

Life Science

Week 1: Day 1 (page 14)
1. d
2. c
3. Possible answer includes, "Because an animal's home doesn't affect whether or not they have a backbone."

Week 1: Day 2 (page 15)
1. c
2. d
3. Possible answer includes, "Mammals have live births."

Week 1: Day 3 (page 16)
1. b
2. c
3. Possible answer includes, "Did the animal have wings?"
4. Possible answer includes, "Dinosaur."

Week 1: Day 4 (page 17)
1. c
2. a
3. Possible answer includes, "Build a model of an animal by using a pipe cleaner and beads for the backbone, and adding legs and a head."

Week 1: Day 5 (page 18)
Mammals: lion, cow, dog
Birds: eagle, raven
Reptiles: snake, turtle, alligator
Amphibians: frog, salamander
Fish: salmon, catfish
Invertebrates: jellyfish, ant, spider

Week 2: Day 1 (page 19)
1. d
2. c
3. Possible answer includes, "A dog is a terrestrial pet. A fish is an aquatic pet."
4. Amphibian

Week 2: Day 2 (page 20)
1. a
2. b
3. Possible answer includes, "Young amphibians breathe with gills and live in water. Adult amphibians breathe with lungs and live mostly on land."

Week 2: Day 3 (page 21)
1. a
2. c
3. Possible answer includes, "Does it have legs or fins?"

Week 2: Day 4 (page 22)
1. b
2. a
3. Possible answer includes, "Research the answer in books, or ask an employee at a pet store."

Week 2: Day 5 (page 23)
Aquatic: dolphin, jellyfish
Terrestrial: ant, deer, monkey, wolf
On land and water: frog, newt
1. Possible answer includes, "They can live in water and on land."

Week 3: Day 1 (page 24)
1. b
2. c
3. Possible answer includes, "To absorb water and nutrients from the soil."

Week 3: Day 2 (page 25)
1. b
2. d
3. Possible answer includes, "To support the plant, and to collect nutrients and water from the soil."

Week 3: Day 3 (page 26)
1. b
2. b
3. Possible answer includes, "How do these roots function differently?"

Week 3: Day 4 (page 27)
1. c
2. d
3. Possible answer includes, "He could make sure that both plants are getting the same amount of sunlight."
4. Possible answer includes, "Yes, because plants need sunlight to make food."

Answer Key (cont.)

Week 3: Day 5 (page 28)

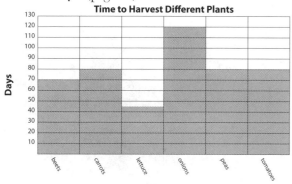

Time to Harvest Different Plants

1. Carrots

Week 4: Day 1 (page 29)
1. b
2. d
3. Possible answer includes, "Because the prey cannot see the predators coming as easily."
4. Diurnal because they sleep at night.

Week 4: Day 2 (page 30)
1. c
2. b
3. Possible answer includes, "Thick fur to stay warm and large eyes to see well."

Week 4: Day 3 (page 31)
1. c
2. c
3. Possible animal includes, "What do nocturnal animals do at night?"
4. Possible answer includes, "Yes because nocturnal animals prefer to be active at night."

Week 4: Day 4 (page 32)
1. d
2. d
3. Possible answer includes, "Playing music to keep the bats awake, turning off the lights, and feeding the bats during the day."
4. Possible answer includes, "Find a mate, eat, and fly around."

Week 4: Day 5 (page 33)
Nocturnal: bat, owl, raccoon
Diurnal: dog, cow
1. Possible answer includes, "Hearing and sense of smell because they help the animal find food."
2. Possible answer includes, "Their hearing is not as good as nocturnal animals."

Week 5: Day 1 (page 34)
1. b
2. d
3. a

Week 5: Day 2 (page 35)
1. d
2. c
3. b

Week 5: Day 3 (page 36)
1. a
2. a
3. Possible answer includes, "If it was missing fewer feathers, could it fly?"
4. Possible answer includes, "Yes, because the bird needs its tail to steer."

Week 5: Day 4 (page 37)
1. a
2. a
3. Possible answer includes, "The model of the arm can have five fingers, and the model of the wing can have two."

Week 5: Day 5 (page 38)

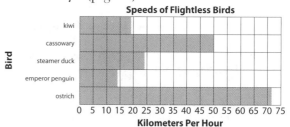

Speeds of Flightless Birds

1. Possible answer includes, "No, because people cannot run that fast."

Week 6: Day 1 (page 39)
1. c
2. a
3. a
4. Possible answer includes, "No, because animals need legs to escape predators."

Week 6: Day 2 (page 40)
1. c
2. b
3. a

Answer Key *(cont.)*

Week 6: Day 3 (page 41)

1. d
2. a
3. Possible answer includes, "How strong are a giraffe's bones?"
4. Possible answer includes, "To reach food."

Week 6: Day 4 (page 42)

1. c
2. a
3. Possible answer includes, "Rob can read a book about stick insects."

Week 6: Day 5 (page 43)

Possible answers include:
Human: walk upright, play sports, dance
Giraffe: reach food, support its body, run from predators
Stick Insect: blend in, escape predators, catch food

Week 7: Day 1 (page 44)

1. b
2. c
3. c

Week 7: Day 2 (page 45)

1. b
2. d
3. Possible answer includes, "Because they don't have lungs."

Week 7: Day 3 (page 46)

1. b
2. a
3. Possible answer includes, "Why can't fish gills get oxygen from air?"
4. Possible answer includes, "Yes, because they need gills to breathe underwater."

Week 7: Day 4 (page 47)

1. d
2. b
3. Possible answer includes, "Ask a pet store employee or research it online."
4. Possible answer includes, "Yes, because different fish might need different amounts of oxygen."

Week 7: Day 5 (page 48)

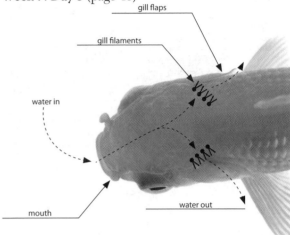

1. Possible answer includes, "It would die because fish cannot breathe in air."

Week 8: Day 1 (page 49)

1. a
2. c
3. d

Week 8: Day 2 (page 50)

1. b
2. a
3. d

Week 8: Day 3 (page 51)

1. b
2. a
3. Possible answer includes, "What parts of the raccoon's eyes are different?"
4. Possible answer includes, "Owls. Yes, I think their eyes are more sensitive."

Week 8: Day 4 (page 52)

1. a
2. a
3. Possible answer includes, "She can choose toys that contrast with the floor."

Answer Key *(cont.)*

Week 8: Day 5 (page 53)

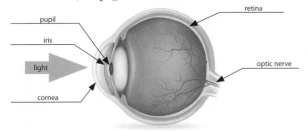

1. Pupil
2. To let in more light.
3. Possible answer includes, "Protecting the eye because it is the outer layer of the eye."

Week 9: Day 1 (page 54)

1. c
2. a
3. c
4. Possible answer includes, "It would have a hard time finding food because it relies on its sense of smell to find food."

Week 9: Day 2 (page 55)

1. a
2. b
3. b
4. a

Week 9: Day 3 (page 56)

1. a
2. a
3. Possible answer includes, "How do smells stick to the snake's tongue?"
4. Possible answer includes, "Yes because scents might stick to their tongue that people can't smell."

Week 9: Day 4 (page 57)

1. b
2. a
3. Possible answer includes, "Hide her food bowl and see if she can find it."

Week 9: Day 5 (page 58)

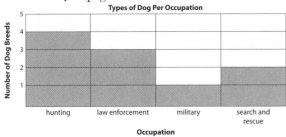

1. Hunting is most common. Military is least common.

Week 10: Day 1 (page 59)

1. a
2. c
3. b

Week 10: Day 2 (page 60)

1. b
2. a
3. b

Week 10: Day 3 (page 61)

1. c
2. a
3. Possible answer includes, "Does Mika's ear have an injury or infection?"
4. Possible answer includes, "Take the cat to the vet."

Week 10: Day 4 (page 62)

1. b
2. b
3. Possible answer includes, "Blow the whistle and see if the dog reacts."
4. Answers will vary.

Week 10: Day 5 (page 63)

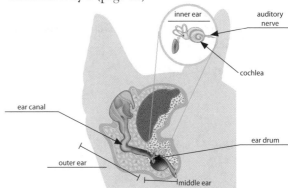

1. Answers will vary but should include the following components: sound enters the ear, the ear drum vibrates, the vibrations travel through the ear, the auditory nerve sends signals to the brain, and the brain converts signals to sound.
2. Possible answer includes, "Yes because people have the same ear parts."

Week 11: Day 1 (page 64)

1. d
2. b
3. Possible answer includes, "The deer population could become too large."
4. Possible answer includes, "Rabbits dig holes in the ground."

Answer Key (cont.)

Week 11: Day 2 (page 65)

1. c
2. b
3. Possible answer includes: "Certain animals would not have homes."

Week 11: Day 3 (page 66)

1. c
2. a
3. Possible answer includes, "What will happen to the forest if the deer eat too many plants?"

Week 11: Day 4 (page 67)

1. d
2. c
3. Possible answer includes, "Read a book about beaver dams."

Week 11: Day 5 (page 68)

Drawings will vary but should include a dam, pond, and animals.

1. Answers will vary.

Week 12: Day 1 (page 69)

1. c
2. c
3. Possible answer includes, "It could force animals to move and kill plants."

Week 12: Day 2 (page 70)

1. a
2. b
3. b

Week 12: Day 3 (page 71)

1. b
2. d
3. Possible answer includes, "How will these trees help the town?"
4. Possible answer includes, "He could pick up trash."

Week 12: Day 4 (page 72)

1. a
2. a
3. Possible answers include, "Compost," "Plant trees," or "Take the bus."

Week 12: Day 5 (page 73)

Drawings will vary.

1. Possible answer includes, "Because we only have one Earth. Some changes can have a negative effect on Earth."

Physical Science

Week 1: Day 1 (page 74)

1. b
2. b
3. b
4. a
5. The ball that is rolling quickly because the faster something moves, the more kinetic energy it has.

Week 1: Day 2 (page 75)

1. b
2. a
3. a
4. Possible answer includes, "The faster the ball is rolling, the less time it takes to reach the bottom of the ramp."

Week 1: Day 3 (page 76)

1. a
2. Possible answer includes, "No, because it would not have enough energy to go up the hills."
3. Possible answer includes, "How high can I make the hills?"
4. Potential energy

Week 1: Day 4 (page 77)

1. b
2. a
3. Possible answer includes, "Make the hill smaller."

Week 1: Day 5 (page 78)

Drawings should show a track that has hills shorter than the starting point.

1. Answers will vary.

Week 2: Day 1 (page 79)

1. a
2. b
3. c
4. Possible answer includes, "Pull the car back as far as possible before letting it go."

Week 2: Day 2 (page 80)

1. b
2. d
3. b

Answer Key (cont.)

Week 2: Day 3 (page 81)
1. a
2. b
3. Possible answer includes, "What would happen if I pushed the car harder?"
4. Possible answer includes, "Yes, because it is harder for things to roll on certain surfaces."

Week 2: Day 4 (page 82)
1. a
2. b
3. Possible answers include, "Put the cars on a slope," "Change the floor, " or "Push harder."
4. Possible answer includes, "Yes because the weights might be different."

Week 2: Day 5 (page 83)

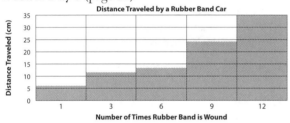

1. Possible answer includes, "If the car is pushed as well as wound."
2. Possible answer includes, "Yes, because a car would roll faster down a ramp."

Week 3: Day 1 (page 84)
1. a
2. d
3. c

Week 3: Day 2 (page 85)
1. b
2. c
3. c

Week 3: Day 3 (page 86)
1. b
2. c
3. Possible answer includes, "Will the heat lamps cook the food or just keep it warm once it is already hot?"
4. Possible answer includes, "They keep the food warm before the waiters take it to the tables."

Week 3: Day 4 (page 87)
1. d
2. a
3. Possible answer includes, "Research different types of heat lamps and what works best for reptiles."
4. Possible answers include, "To keep food warm," or "To keep other animals warm."

Week 3: Day 5 (page 88)

heat energy · light energy · filament · electrical energy

1. Answer should include: electricity heats the filament and is converted to heat and light.
2. Possible answer includes, "It would be hot."
3. Possible answers include: lamp, fish tank, and flashlight.

Week 4: Day 1 (page 89)
1. c
2. c
3. a
4. Possible answer includes, "Yes, because the cone would move while the speaker is playing music."
5. Possible answer includes, "No, because it wouldn't be loud enough to hear."

Week 4: Day 2 (page 90)
1. c
2. b
3. a

Week 4: Day 3 (page 91)
1. b
2. b
3. Possible answer includes, "How does the battery power the headphones?"
4. Possible answer includes, "Cell phones, radios, and toys."

Answer Key *(cont.)*

Week 4: Day 4 (page 92)

1. b
2. a
3. Possible answer includes, "Look it up on the Internet or read a book."
4. Possible answer includes, "It would not make sound."

Week 4: Day 5 (page 93)

Uses electricity to make sound: headphones, speakers, radio, television

Does not use electricity to make sound: flute, tambourine, trumpet, animals

1. Possible answer includes, "Electricity makes the vibrations."

Week 5: Day 1 (page 94)

1. b
2. a
3. d

Week 5: Day 2 (page 95)

1. a
2. a
3. Possible answer includes, "Electricity powers the fan and turns into movement. It also heats the wires and turns into heat. Hot air blows out and evaporates water from your hair."
4. Possible answer includes, "Space heaters, toasters, and ovens."

Week 5: Day 3 (page 96)

1. c
2. c
3. Possible answer includes, "How do different objects things convert electricity to heat?"
4. Possible answer includes, "Oven and fryer,"

Week 5: Day 4 (page 97)

1. b
2. a
3. Possible answer includes, "She could explore all the different objects in her house that make heat."
4. Possible answer includes, "Kinetic energy. The movement of your hands turns into heat."

Week 5: Day 5 (page 98)

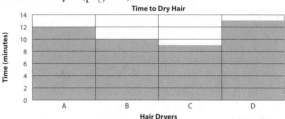

1. Hair Dryer C because it takes the least amount of time to dry hair.

Week 6: Day 1 (page 99)

1. d
2. a
3. c
4. Possible answer includes, "The fast ball would cause a loud noise, and the pins would move far. The slow ball would cause a quieter noise, and the pins wouldn't move as far."

Week 6: Day 2 (page 100)

1. c
2. a
3. Possible answer includes, "It transfers more energy."

Week 6: Day 3 (page 101)

1. a
2. b
3. Possible answer includes, "What will happen if I change the angle of the ruler?"

Week 6: Day 4 (page 102)

1. d
2. b
3. Possible answers include, "Marcy tries the ruler at three different heights," or, "Marcy tries the marble at three different placements on the ruler."

Week 6: Day 5 (page 103)

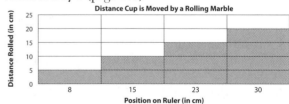

Answer Key *(cont.)*

Week 7: Day 1 (page 104)
1. d
2. a
3. b
4. Possible answer includes, "The tennis ball would change directions because the bowling ball is heavier."

Week 7: Day 2 (page 105)
1. c
2. a
3. Possible answer includes, "No, because the energy transfer would be different than when the balls weigh the same amount. The heavier ball would transfer more energy to the lighter ball."
4. Possible answer includes, "The kinetic energy is transferred to the unmoving ball."

Week 7: Day 3 (page 106)
1. c
2. Possible answer includes, "I think Marcus's car will change direction because it is lighter. The heavier car will transfer more energy to the lighter car."
3. Possible answer includes, "How would the size of the car affect the collision if both cars are the same weight and are going the same speed?"

Week 7: Day 4 (page 107)
1. d
2. Possible answer includes, "Yes, because the two cars will no longer be moving the same speed."
3. Possible answer includes, "They need to do at least three trials of each scenario and change only one variable at a time."

Week 7: Day 5 (page 108)
Drawings and answers will vary. They should show balls changing direction appropriately for the weights and directions they are traveling.
1. Answers will vary, but students should mention energy transfer.
2. Answers will vary, but students should describe an appropriate change to their scenario.

Week 8: Day 1 (page 109)
1. b
2. a
3. Possible answer includes, "They are inexpensive."

Week 8: Day 2 (page 110)
1. c
2. b
3. d

Week 8: Day 3 (page 111)
1. b
2. a
3. Possible answer includes, "Would you rather have fewer, more efficient bulbs or more, less efficient bulbs?"

Week 8: Day 4 (page 112)
1. a
2. c
3. 1 LED, 3 CFL, 1 incandescent. This is the most efficient combination that he can get while still buying five bulbs.
4. Possible answer includes, "As many LED bulbs as possible because they are much more efficient."

Week 8: Day 5 (page 113)

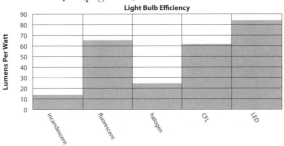

1. Possible answer includes, "Fluorescent and CFL because they are the next most efficient."

Week 9: Day 1 (page 114)
1. a
2. d
3. b

Week 9: Day 2 (page 115)
1. b
2. a
3. No, because you have to measure between the same two points.
4. No, because the amplitude is measured from the middle of the wave to the crest.

Week 9: Day 3 (page 116)
1. c
2. d
3. Possible answer includes, "Is there a way to build a wave model that will move?"

Answer Key *(cont.)*

Week 9: Day 4 (page 117)
1. a
2. b
3. Possible answer includes, "She could build a wave model with water."
4. Possible answer includes, "String or clay"

Week 9: Day 5 (page 118)
Drawings should include accurate labels for crest, trough, wavelength, and amplitude.
1. Possible answer includes, "Sound, light, and water."
2. Possible answer includes, "Yes, because the wave's energy can be transferred to other things."

Week 10: Day 1 (page 119)
1. a
2. c
3. Possible answer includes, "No, you can send Morse Code messages with light."

Week 10: Day 2 (page 120)
1. c
2. a
3. Possible answer includes, "The number one is the opposite of the number nine."
4. Possible answer includes, "B is 3 dots and a dash. Y is 3 dashes and a dot. C is 2 dots and 2 dashes. X is also 2 dots and 2 dashes."

Week 10: Day 3 (page 121)
1. d
2. a
3. Possible answer includes, "What other ways could I represent dots and dashes?"
4. Possible answer includes, "Flash light and car horn."

Week 10: Day 4 (page 122)
1. b
2. a
3. Possible answer includes, "The best time to use light is when it can be easily seen. The best time to use sound is if the recipient of the message is too far to see light or if it's too bright to see light."

Week 10: Day 5 (page 123)
Answers will vary.
1. Answers will vary. Items could include flashlights, horns, window blinds.

Week 11: Day 1 (page 124)
1. c
2. a
3. c

Week 11: Day 2 (page 125)
1. a
2. b
3. Possible answers include, "Internet connections are decoded by modems," "Barcodes are decoded by scanners," or "Television is decoded by a TV."

Week 11: Day 3 (page 126)
1. b
2. a
3. Possible answer includes, "What are all the different ways I can send messages over a long distance? What is the easiest?"
4. Possible answer includes, "Cell phone and computer."

Week 11: Day 4 (page 127)
1. b
2. a
3. Possible answer includes, "Text message and instant messaging."

Week 11: Day 5 (page 128)
Drawings will vary.
1. Answers will vary.
2. If the answer includes digital communication, the message should not lose quality when it gets to the recipient. If the messagage is using a loud sound or light to send a message, the message could degrade.

Week 12: Day 1 (page 129)
1. a
2. c
3. Possible answer includes, "Because they reflect all the light."

Week 12: Day 2 (page 130)
1. d
2. b
3. b

Week 12: Day 3 (page 131)
1. c
2. d
3. Possible answer includes, "Will a mirror always reflect all light?"

Week 12: Day 4 (page 132)
1. a
2. b
3. Possible answer includes, "She could shine the light at different objects and take notes about the results."

Answer Key *(cont.)*

Week 12: Day 5 (page 133)

An arrow should point from the light source to the object. The second arrow should point from the object to the eye.

1. Possible answer includes, "Because there is no light to reflect off of objects. We need light to see."

Earth and Space Science

Week 1: Day 1 (page 134)

1. b
2. c
3. b

Week 1: Day 2 (page 135)

1. b
2. a
3. c
4. Possible answer includes "Yes, because the earth moves a lot at fault lines."

Week 1: Day 3 (page 136)

1. a
2. c
3. On the edges of tectonic plates.
4. Possible answer includes, "What causes them to move?"

Week 1: Day 4 (page 137)

1. d
2. a
3. Possible answer includes, "Shake the doll house back and forth."
4. Possible answer includes, "Minor because minor earthquakes don't cause damage."

Week 1: Day 5 (page 138)

1. Possible answer includes, "Because there is a major fault line in California."
2. Possible answer includes, "Yes, because there is a major fault line there."

Week 2: Day 1 (page 139)

1. b
2. c
3. b
4. Possible answer includes, "They form in different ways."

Week 2: Day 2 (page 140)

1. a
2. b
3. c
4. c

Week 2: Day 3 (page 141)

1. c
2. b
3. Possible answer includes, "What event happened for the igneous rock to be deposited? What happened to the creatures that lived before that event?"

Week 2: Day 4 (page 142)

1. a
2. a
3. Answers will vary but should include different layers representing different types of rock.

Week 2: Day 5 (page 143)

Drawings will vary but should include several layers with the bottom layer labeled "oldest," and the top layer labeled "newest."

1. Answers will vary.
2. Possible answer includes, "Underwater."

Week 3: Day 1 (page 144)

1. b
2. a
3. Possible answer includes, "No, it is usually just the bone that becomes fossilized."

Week 3: Day 2 (page 145)

1. a
2. b
3. Possible answer includes, "No, they are more like stone because minerals fill the pores of the bone."

Week 3: Day 3 (page 146)

1. a
2. c
3. Possible answer includes, "What animal left the fossil?"
4. Possible answer includes, "Because it is a large job that needs many people."

Week 3: Day 4 (page 147)

1. b
2. c
3. Possible answer includes, "It would be older because layers are deposited from the bottom up."
4. Possible answer includes, "No, because it wouldn't narrow down the age range of other fossils very much."

Answer Key *(cont.)*

Week 3: Day 5 (page 148)
1. G is the newest because it is on the top. A is the oldest because it is on the bottom.
2. You could use C to help with relative dating. Layer C is 300 million years old. The fossils below it could be 400 million years old, and the fossils above it could be 200 million years old.

Week 4: Day 1 (page 149)
1. a
2. c
3. Possible answer includes, "Cut down trees."

Week 4: Day 2 (page 150)
1. c
2. a
3. Possible answer includes, "It could collapse."
4. Possible answer includes, "Wind or ice."

Week 4: Day 3 (page 151)
1. a
2. a
3. Possible answer includes, "How to plants prevent erosion?"
4. Possible answer includes, "Plant grass."

Week 4: Day 4 (page 152)
1. a
2. a
3. Possible answer includes, "A large crop of oats because their roots would cover more ground than a single tree."
4. Possible answer includes, "Research in reliable sources."

Week 4: Day 5 (page 153)
Answers will vary. Pictures should clearly show erosion.

Week 5: Day 1 (page 154)
1. c
2. d
3. a

Week 5: Day 2 (page 155)
1. b
2. a
3. Possible answer includes, "It will become wider."

Week 5: Day 3 (page 156)
1. a
2. b
3. Possible answer includes, "How does water erode something that is so hard?"
4. Possible answer includes, "More shallow because erosion has made it deeper over time."

Week 5: Day 4 (page 157)
1. a
2. d
3. Possible answer includes, "Alexander can research the average rate of beach erosion and compare Louisiana's rate."

Week 5: Day 5 (page 158)

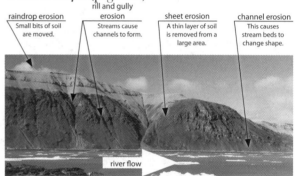

1. Possible answer includes, "The hill will become flatter."
2. Possible answer includes, "There will be more channels in the hill."

Week 6: Day 1 (page 159)
1. c
2. a
3. Possible answer includes, "Yes, because erosion will change them."
4. Possible answer includes, "Because it can blow away topsoil on farms."

Week 6: Day 2 (page 160)
1. b
2. a
3. Possible answer includes, "It will erode all of the soil."
4. Possible answer includes, "Erosion decreases as ground cover increases."

Week 6: Day 3 (page 161)
1. a
2. c
3. Possible answer includes, "Why do the rocks erode into arches?"

Answer Key *(cont.)*

Week 6: Day 4 (page 162)
1. a
2. a
3. Possible answer includes, "Use a hair dryer."
4. Possible answer includes, "Yes, because the objects would help hold the soil in place."

Week 6: Day 5 (page 163)
Drawings will vary.
2. Answers will vary but should reflect that the student understands erosion is a long process.

Week 7: Day 1 (page 164)
1. c
2. a
3. c

Week 7: Day 2 (page 165)
1. b
2. a
3. The contour lines are close together.

Week 7: Day 3 (page 166)
1. c
2. a
3. Possible answer includes, "What is the best way to plan a hike with a topographic map?"
4. Possible answer includes "It will help them know where the hills and valleys are."

Week 7: Day 4 (page 167)
1. a
2. b
3. Possible answer includes, "Jenny can decide how high they want to hike and plan a route that keeps that elevation in mind."
4. Possible answer includes, "Yes, because it will tell her how steep the land is."

Week 7: Day 5 (page 168)
Labeled maps and answers will vary.

Week 8: Day 1 (page 169)
1. b
2. d
3. Possible answer includes, "A large slab of Earth's crust that moves."
4. Possible answer includes, "Where several fault lines wrap around the Pacific Ocean. There are many volcanoes and earthquakes there."

Week 8: Day 2 (page 170)
1. b
2. a
3. volcanoes

Week 8: Day 3 (page 171)
1. a
2. Possible answer includes, "Large and red because it would draw attention to it."
3. Possible answer includes, "Why are there so many volcanoes in Alaska?"

Week 8: Day 4 (page 172)
1. b
2. a
3. Possible answer includes, "Jose could look up what the orange triangle with an eye means to find out the status of the volcano."

Week 8: Day 5 (page 173)

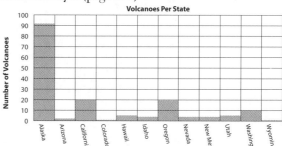

1. California, Oregon, and Washington

Week 9: Day 1 (page 174)
1. d
2. a
3. d
4. Possible answer includes, "They can hurt animals by taking away their homes."

Week 9: Day 2 (page 175)
1. c
2. a
3. c
4. Possible answer includes, "To buildings and houses."

Week 9: Day 3 (page 176)
1. b
2. b
3. Possible answer includes, "How can I make it stronger?"

Answer Key (cont.)

Week 9: Day 4 (page 177)

1. a
2. c
3. Possible answer includes, "He could research dams in books at the library."
4. Possible answer includes "Yes, because other animals might need those animals to live."

Week 9: Day 5 (page 178)

Positive: provides water for irrigation, makes hydroelectric power, creates lakes for recreation, supply drinking water, can prevent flooding

Negative: changes animal habitats, can cause flooding in flat basins, can make land less fertile downstream

Week 10: Day 1 (page 179)

1. d
2. a
3. b
4. Possible answer includes, "It goes to power lines that carry electricity to buildings."

Week 10: Day 2 (page 180)

1. a
2. b
3. d

Week 10: Day 3 (page 181)

1. b
2. a
3. Possible answer includes, "Could I use the turning pinwheel to create electricity?"
4. Possible answer includes, "Kites or toy sail boats."

Week 10: Day 4 (page 182)

1. a
2. c
3. Answers vary but should include using the candy for wheels and the paper for a sail.
4. Possible answer includes, "The volcano could erupt at any time."

Week 10: Day 5 (page 183)

Step 1: blades of the wind turbine
Step 2: generators, electricity
Step 3: buildings

1. Possible answer includes, "Lights in a house, air conditioning, and appliances."
2. Yes, because it never runs out.

Week 11: Day 1 (page 184)

1. d
2. d
3. Possible answer includes, "They can use early warning systems."
4. Possible answer includes, "Because people have limited time to get out of the flood zone."

Week 11: Day 2 (page 185)

1. c
2. a
3. Possible answer includes, "Outdoor sirens."

Week 11: Day 3 (page 186)

1. c
2. Possible answer includes, "Warnings on the radio and TV."
3. Possible answer includes, "What kind of warning systems are already in place?"

Week 11: Day 4 (page 187)

1. a
2. d
3. Possible answer includes, "Create a series of TV commercials to educate people."

Week 11: Day 5 (page 188)

Drawings and answers will vary.

Week 12: Day 1 (page 189)

1. c
2. b
3. Possible answer includes, "It means that the volcano could erupt any time because it is overdue."

Week 12: Day 2 (page 190)

1. a
2. b
3. Possible answer includes, "The volcano could erupt at any time."

Week 12: Day 3 (page 191)

1. a
2. c
3. Possible answer includes, "How do you read the information from a seismometer?"
4. Possible answer includes, "A tall line because it shows a greater change in movement."

Answer Key *(cont.)*

Week 12: Day 4 (page 192)

1. a
2. a
3. Possible answer includes, "He could suspend the house on string."

Week 12: Day 5 (page 193)

1. Possible answer includes, "The building without base isolation moves a lot more."
2. Possible answer includes, "It keeps it separate from the moving ground, and it stops it from shaking as much."
3. Possible answer includes, "They reduce damage to buildings."

Human Leg Diagram

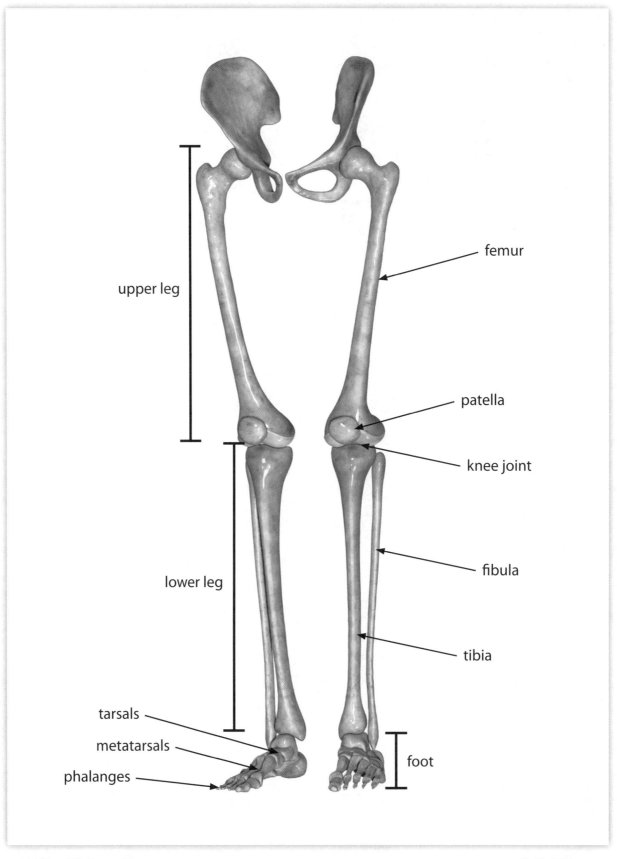

upper leg

femur

patella

knee joint

lower leg

fibula

tibia

tarsals

metatarsals

phalanges

foot

Tectonic Plates

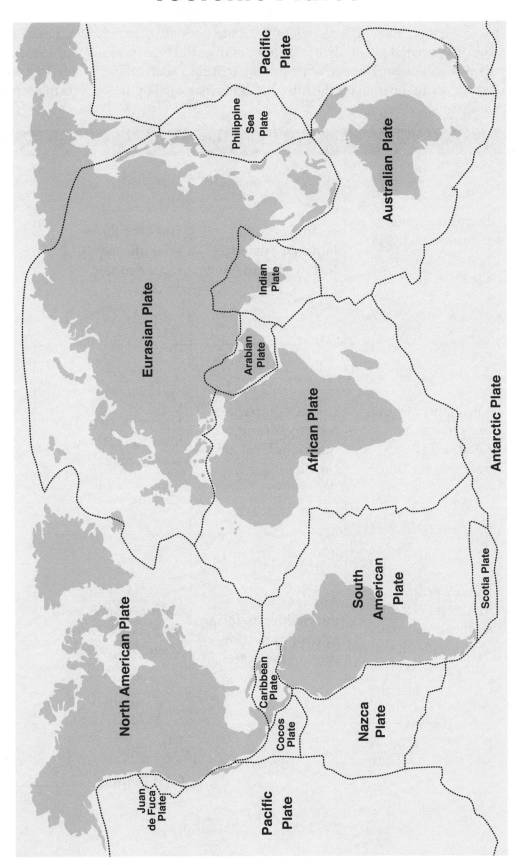

Student Name: _____ Date: _____

Developing Questions Rubric

Directions: Complete this rubric every four weeks to evaluate students' Day 3 activity sheets. Only one rubric is needed per student. Their work over the four weeks can be evaluated together. Evaluate their work in each category by writing a score in each row. Then, add up their scores, and write the total on the line. Students may earn up to 5 points in each row and up to 15 points total.

Skill	5	3	1	Score
Forming Scientific Inquiries	Forms scientific inquiries related to text all or nearly all the time.	Forms scientific inquiries related to text most of the time.	Does not form scientific inquiries related to text.	
Interpreting Text	Correctly interprets texts to answer questions all or nearly all the time.	Correctly interprets texts to answer questions most of the time.	Does not correctly interpret texts to answer questions.	
Applying Information	Applies new information to form scientific questions all or nearly all the time.	Applies new information to form scientific questions most of the time.	Does not apply new information to form scientific questions.	

Total Points: _____

Planning Solutions Rubric

Directions: Complete this rubric every four weeks to evaluate students' Day 4 activity sheets. Only one rubric is needed per student. Their work over the four weeks can be evaluated together. Evaluate their work in each category by writing a score in each row. Then, add up their scores, and write the total on the line. Students may earn up to 5 points in each row and up to 15 points total.

Skill	5	3	1	Score
Planning Investigations	Plans reasonable investigations to study topics all or nearly all the time.	Plans reasonable investigations to study topics most of the time.	Does not plan reasonable investigations to study topics.	
Making Predictions	Studies events to make reasonable predictions all or nearly all the time.	Studies events to make reasonable predictions most of the time.	Does not study events to make reasonable predictions.	
Choosing Next Steps	Chooses reasonable next steps for investigations all or nearly all the time.	Chooses reasonable next steps for investigations most of the time.	Does not choose reasonable next steps for investigations.	

Total Points: _____

Communicating Results Rubric

Directions: Complete this rubric every four weeks to evaluate students' Day 5 activity sheets. Only one rubric is needed per student. Their work over the four weeks can be evaluated together. Evaluate their work in each category by writing a score in each row. Then, add up their scores, and write the total on the line. Students may earn up to 5 points in each row and up to 15 points total.

Skill	5	3	1	Score
Representing Data	Correctly represents data with charts and graphs all or nearly all the time.	Correctly represents data with charts and graphs most of the time.	Does not correctly represents data with charts and graphs.	
Making Connections	Makes reasonable connections between new information and prior knowledge all or nearly all the time.	Makes reasonable connections between new information and prior knowledge most of the time.	Does not make reasonable connections between new information and prior knowledge.	
Explaining Results	Uses evidence to accurately explain results all or nearly all the time.	Uses evidence to accurately explain results most of the time.	Does not use evidence to accurately explain results.	

Total Points: _____

Life Science Analysis Chart

Directions: Record the total of each student's Day 1 and Day 2 scores from the four weeks. Then, record each student's rubric scores (pages 210–212). Add the totals, and record the sums in the Total Scores column. Record the average class score in the last row.

Student Name	Week 4					Week 8					Week 12					Total Scores
	Day 1	Day 2	DQ	PS	CR	Day 1	Day 2	DQ	PS	CR	Day 1	Day 2	DQ	PS	CR	
Average Classroom Score																

DQ = Developing Questions, PS = Planning Solutions, CR = Communicating Results

Physical Science Analysis Chart

Directions: Record the total of each student's Day 1 and Day 2 scores from the four weeks. Then, record each student's rubric scores (pages 210–212). Add the totals, and record the sums in the Total Scores column. Record the average class score in the last row.

Student Name	Week 4					Week 8					Week 12					Total Scores
	Day 1	Day 2	DQ	PS	CR	Day 1	Day 2	DQ	PS	CR	Day 1	Day 2	DQ	PS	CR	
Average Classroom Score																

DQ = Developing Questions, PS = Planning Solutions, CR = Communicating Results

Earth and Space Science Analysis Chart

Directions: Record the total of each student's Day 1 and Day 2 scores from the four weeks. Then, record each student's rubric scores (pages 210–212). Add the totals, and record the sums in the Total Scores column. Record the average class score in the last row.

Student Name	Week 4 Day 1	Day 2	DQ	PS	CR	Week 8 Day 1	Day 2	DQ	PS	CR	Week 12 Day 1	Day 2	DQ	PS	CR	Total Scores
Average Classroom Score																

DQ = Developing Questions, PS = Planning Solutions, CR = Communicating Results

Digital Resources

To access digital resources, go to this website and enter the following code: 34888543
www.teachercreatedmaterials.com/administrators/download-files/

Rubrics

Resource	Filename
Developing Questions Rubric	questionsrubric.pdf
Planning Solutions Rubric	solutionsrubric.pdf
Communicating Results Rubric	resultsrubric.pdf

Item Analysis Sheets

Resource	Filename
Life Science Analysis Chart	LSanalysischart.pdf
	LSanalysischart.docx
	LSanalysischart.xlsx
Physical Science Analysis Chart	PSanalysischart.pdf
	PSanalysischart.docx
	PSanalysischart.xlsx
Earth and Space Science Analysis Chart	ESSanalysischart.pdf
	ESSanalysischart.docx
	ESSanalysischart.xlsx

Standards

Resource	Filename
Standards Charts	standards.pdf